WORD ABUSE

By Donna Woolfolk Cross

SPEAKING OF WORDS
WORD ABUSE: HOW THE WORDS WE USE USE US

WORD ABUSE

How the words we use use us

Donna Woolfolk Cross

Introduction by
William Woolfolk

COWARD, McCANN & GEOGHEGAN, INC.
NEW YORK

Library of Congress Cataloging in Publication Data

Cross, Donna Woolfolk.
  Word abuse.

  1. English language in the United States.
2. English language—Jargon. 3. English
Language—Social aspects. 4. Lexicology—
Popular works. I. Title.
PE2834.C7   301.2'1   78-11025
ISBN 0-698-10906-6 cloth
      0-698-10968-6 paper

Printed in the United States of America

Acknowledgments

Special and affectionate thanks go to my husband Richard, who patiently sacrificed my attention at home while I anguished over this book, and who never once faltered in his devotion, support, sanity, laughter, and love . . . my mother, Dorothy Woolfolk, who believed in me, and who took time away from her own writing to help in the final editing of this book . . . Thomas Friedmann, who read the manuscript and made many helpful suggestions . . . James Mackillop, who generously supplied several of the clippings and articles cited here . . . Yvonne Hudgins, Nina Terris, Cindy Coon, and Judy Geyer, who spent many long hours entertaining my baby daughter so I could work uninterruptedly . . . Ellen Coin and Barbara Linzer, who provided material for the chapter on the language of the law . . . Lil Kinney, Frank Doble, and the entire library staff at Onondaga Community College, who gave so generously of their time and expertise in researching material for this book. . . . Finally, to my daughter, Emily, without whom this book would have been written three years ago and would by now be out of print.

For my father, William Woolfolk,

*without whom neither this book nor its author
would have been possible*

Table of Contents

WORD ABUSE

Lament and Introduction

William Woolfolk

I'll tell you what is discouraging.

What is discouraging is to discover your daughter knows more than you do.

Part of the joy of being a father is dandling a daughter on your knee while instructing her in some mystery of the universe. (If you have a son, there is less knee-dandling and more instruction in how to throw a curve ball or a slider.) For a while you have a worshipful audience, entirely willing to believe everything you tell her.

Trouble begins when your daughter starts going to school. Most fathers get through the early years, say up to around the fifth or sixth grade. Your daughter comes home full of geography and arithmetic and spelling, but you can nod sagely and chime in with a piece of information that she hasn't heard yet in class. This will give the impression that you know just a little bit more than she does. Your fund of knowledge is mysterious, like the information stored in the memory banks of a computer. She can push a button and get something back she

11

doesn't know, and she has no way of guessing how much unrequested wisdom is stored in there.

High school is a real problem. Even if you remember what you learned in high school, your information is out of date. The first time your daughter sets you straight, a cloud forms no bigger than a teacher's hand. She may overlook the first slip, the second, even the third, but somewhere along the way a terrible truth is going to break upon her: Daddy is not Solomon. Very soon afterward she learns that Daddy would probably not pass her high school final exam. (It helps a little if you can point out that Solomon probably wouldn't either.)

Abandon hope when she enters college. All college students pick up some strange virus that decreases respect for their elders. A father can hold his own only if he is fast on his feet, does surreptitious reading before having any serious discussion, and, as a last resort, stands up for the enduring values of sturdy common sense and experience.

Now let me descend from the general to my particular dilemma. My daughter chose a field of knowledge in which to specialize and, luckily for me, this was a field in which I retain some shards and fragments of knowledge: the English language. I have always tried to write as well as I can. My worst critics (I have no other kind) usually grant me that. When critics are in a really censorious mood, of course, they will grant you nothing.

For a while longer, therefore, I kept calamity at bay. On those happily infrequent occasions when I engaged in intellectual discussions with my daughter, I was able to keep my lips above water. Sometimes a sage comment or two, borrowed from Mark Twain, buoyed me up.

Then one day, while I was not being properly attentive, my ungrateful offspring wrote a textbook. What's more, the textbook was chosen by all sorts of committees. Somewhere along the way, insensibly, she had ceased to be my daughter and become an Authority.

I sat down to read her textbook with more trepidation than

you imagine. Reading any textbook is for me an experience very like wading through swamp gas.

I was most agreeably surprised. There was Authority, to be sure, but *Speaking of Words* (coauthored by James Mackillop: Holt, Rinehart and Winston, 1978) is one of the very few books on language that I would recommend even if it were not written by my daughter. My eyes did not slowly go out of focus. The book made a statement of some importance. The statement is this: Language has its own system of ethics, and any writing that truly communicates is like a small flickering flame in a world of darkness. We must all try to nurture language like that and help it to survive.

Others shared my high opinion of *Speaking of Words*, including Patricia Soliman, the very personable and perceptive editor-in-chief of Coward, McCann & Geoghegan. She suggested that it would be smashing if my daughter and I jointly wrote a popular book on the subject of Word Abuse, the kind of book that would be interesting even to those who think English is something you put on a cue ball. Sounds fine, I said, because after long years of free-lancing, that is what I say when a publisher suggests *anything*.

Although I mostly write novels, this was a topic to which I felt I could contribute because I felt passionately about it. Anyone who abuses words should be condemned to read both volumes of the condensed Oxford Dictionary without the aid of a magnifying glass. Words are our most precious human asset. Humankind made its last great leap forward when we all began to understand what everyone else was saying.

Somehow, our collaboration did not work out as anticipated. Perhaps I can explain why by quoting an excerpt from one of our early discussions. We were talking about a possible introductory chapter on the limitations of different languages, which can sometimes amount to an abuse of meaning.

F: (Having done surreptitious reading) Did you know that the Eskimos have thirty words for snow? Including a word for "falling snow," for "snow on the ground," for "drifting snow" and for "blowing snow." We get along pretty well with just one word "snow." It's hard to figure out why they need so many to say the same thing.

D: It isn't the same thing. People actually perceive things in one language that they can't perceive in another. To an Eskimo, the word "snow" would be practically meaningless. He simply wouldn't get the connection between all the different phenomena so important to his life and the single concept of "snow." Any more than we can understand how the Hopi Indians, who have only one word to describe everything that flies except birds, class an airplane and a mosquito together as *masaytaka.*

F: Oh.

D: The Hopi don't perceive the differences because their vision is limited by using that one word. Just as an Eskimo perceives all the different varieties of snow, partly because he has the words to do it.

F: (weakly) I wouldn't go that far.

D: If you don't believe it, try jotting down in English thirty different kinds of snow—*really* different. Don't cheat with things like artificial snow. I don't think you can get up beyond ten or twelve different kinds.

(A short interval here in which **F** attempts this. He comes up with five.)

F: I'm afraid I can't get beyond twelve either.

D: Most English-speaking people can't. There's

nothing wrong with our eyes. We *see* snow about the same way an Eskimo does; we just don't *perceive* all the things about it that an Eskimo does.

F: (defensively) How many famous Eskimo novelists do you know?

D: There's nothing personal about it, Dad. We can't *perceive* all the things an Eskimo does because we aren't trained to. Our language tells us, in effect, "Don't bother with that. It isn't important."

F: English is *not* an underprivileged language.

D: Of course not. We make many distinctions that an Eskimo doesn't. We make distinctions between types of cars. We distinguish between a Chevrolet and a Jaguar, a Pinto and a Cadillac, a sedan and a sports coupe, between four- and six- and eight-cylinder cars, and front- and rear-wheel-drive cars. For us to call a motorcycle a "car" would be unthinkable. Yet an Eskimo would lump all of these together with lawnmowers under an umbrella word that means something close to "machine."

F: I never learned to speak Eskimo. At least, not fluently.

D: Take the Aztecs. They only had one word for snow, ice, *and* cold. They'd be even more limited than you in describing different varieties of snow.

F: How many famous Aztec novelists do you know?

D: There's nothing *personal* about it, Dad. Snow and ice are clearly different things to us. But the Aztecs didn't see any difference between them because it simply wasn't important for them to see it. And what decided for them it wasn't impor-

D: tant? Their language, which developed over hundreds of years to reflect the reality of their world. Language ends up shaping and defining the world.

F: Right on.

D: Take another example. How many words do you think there are in Arabic for camel?

F: Two. Including dromedary.

D: Six thousand, including the camel's parts and equipment.

F: Six thousand! Homer wrote both the *Iliad* and the *Odyssey* using only nine thousand words. [Adroit use of surreptitious reading—ed.] That measures out to about one and a half camels. It's a waste of time to use six thousand words describing camels when those words could perfectly well be used to describe something else.

D: Again, it's not a question that we can't see these distinctions. Our eyesight is as good as an Arab's. But our language tells us these distinctions aren't important, and so we don't make them.

F: I'll go along with that.

D: Eskimos and Arabs need their snow-and-camel vocabulary to describe a vital part of their lives. We don't need them, so we don't have them. But we do need words that help us cope with our highly complex industrial society. So we have mammoth dictionaries of technical terms. And these words, too, enrich, restrict and control our perceptions. I hope you'll go into that when you write this chapter.

F: Is *this* the chapter I'm going to write?

D: Yes. You should also go into the other ways in which language classifies and defines reality. They aren't all linked to environmental necessity. Some ways seem more arbitrary.

F: Arbitrary?

D: For example, different cultures perceive the color spectrum differently. There doesn't seem to be any environmental necessity for that difference.

F: No, there doesn't.

D: We think everyone sees, as we do, a series of distinct colors. Red and orange and yellow, green, blue and purple. But the Rhodesian natives who speak Shona don't see green and yellow at all. Instead, they have a color called *cicena* which is close to what we would call yellowish-green. To them, what we call "green" is simply dark cicena. And what we call "yellow" is light cicena. Where we see two colors, they only see one.

F: Everybody who speaks Shona must be color blind.

D: They have another color, *cipswuka*, which encompasses every shade from a kind of purplish blue to an orangey red. On the other hand, persons who speak Malay link both black and blue together as *bolong*, and red and brown together as *merah*. And the African Bongo tongue uses one word, *kamaheke*, to describe what we call red and yellow. Liberian natives who speak Bassa have the simplest system of all. They have only two colors, *hui*, which includes all the shades from purple through dark green, and *zizi*, which includes all the rest of the shades from light green through to red.

F: I guess that reflects the backwardness of other languages when it comes to distinguishing colors.

D: Not at all. There are many languages that make *more* color distinctions than we do. Navajo, for instance, distinguishes between shades of black— the black of darkness and the black of coal. The Welsh tongue distinguishes two different types of green.

F: Richard Burton is Welsh.

D: The point is that people who speak different languages see colors a bit differently.

F: Only if they've been drinking.

D: And there's no environmental reason to explain these differences. The languages just happened to evolve that way. Because we speak English, we never see the world as the Shona or the Bassa do—nor even as the Chinese, the Russians or the Indians do.

F: Our book won't sell much in those countries anyway. Although you might be interested to hear that my novels sell as many copies in the Soviet Union as Solzhenitsyn's do.

D: It would be nice if we could adapt for our own use some of the distinctions other languages make. In Chichewa, an East African tongue, there are two past tenses—one for events which continue to have an effect on the present and one for events which do not.

F: That *would* be a useful distinction to make.

D: And the ancient Greeks had the word *opiso*, which meant both "past" and "future," a concept very hard for someone who speaks English to understand. We see ourselves as moving through time, leaving the past behind us and heading for the future. The Greeks thought of themselves as standing still and of *time* as moving, coming up behind them, overtaking them, and becoming the future.

F: Satchel Paige, a famous black baseball pitcher, used to say he never looked back because something might be gaining on him. Does that make him an ancient Greek?

D: He was probably closer to their thinking than we are. Because our language doesn't perceive time as operating in this way, we're likely to dismiss the Greek idea as quaint or eccentric.

F: Maybe you'd better write this chapter.

D: Perhaps you'd rather tell our readers about the kinds of words we don't have in English that we really could use.

F: That's more down my line. I'm always looking for a word that doesn't seem to be in the English language. Finding the right word when you need it is harder than finding an onion pit.

D: You write that chapter, then.

F: The difference between the right word and the almost-right word is the difference between lightning and a lightning bug.

D: I remember. Mark Twain said that.

F: Did he? Well, he was right. Wouldn't it be nice if we could just throw the twenty-six letters of the alphabet on a table and come up with the right word?

D: That's impossible if we don't have the words at all. For instance, we don't have a word to describe the relationship of one mother-in-law to another.

F: How about "trouble"?

D: In fact, we don't perceive the husband's mother and the wife's mother as being really related to *each other*. Imagine the difficulty if one mother-in-law tried to talk about the other. "My son's wife's mother said the most awful thing to me the other day. And what's worse, she had the nerve to say it in my brother's wife's sister's house!"

F: Hmmm.

D: Many languages do have words to describe the relationship of in-laws to each other. As a result, they tend to think of themselves as related in ways that we simply can't. In English, we just have one word to describe relatives of both sexes who are related to us in all kinds of different ways.

F: One word?

D: Cousin. About the only distinction we make is "first cousin," "second cousin," "cousin once removed," etc. You'll come up with lots of other examples, I'm sure.

F: In the novel I'm working on now, I have a scene where a father has to refer to a man his daughter is living with. I didn't know what he'd call him. "My daughter's boy" makes him sound like her son. "Boyfriend" is so old hat that they've started satirizing it. Remember the movie *Young Frankenstein*, where Cloris Leachman makes her dramatic disclosure about her and Baron Frankenstein: "I admit it! I admit it all! He was—he was—my BOYFRIEND!" "Roommate" may get closer to the idea of living together than "boyfriend" does, but you can't be sure if the roommate is of male or female gender. "Lover" is pretty dramatic to describe a young man who happens to be rather staid, conventional, and who shops at Safeway. If I tried using words like "swain," "paramour," "consort" or "mate," I'd be run out of the Realistic Novelist's Guild. Sin-in-law is a possibility, but it's just too cute for my taste. Someone suggested "lover-in-law," but that sounds like the daughter is having an affair with her in-laws.

D: Most of those words do manage to hit thumbs right on the head. Is there a word for two lovers of the same sex who are living together?

F: That would dismay the English language almost as much as it would their parents.

D: Well, you take it from there.

I didn't take it far. I discovered that English could really use an appropriate salutation for a letter addressed to a man and a woman. This happened because I sat down to write an imploring letter to the editors of the magazine that owed me money. One editor is a man, the other a woman. How should I address them? "Dear Gentlemen" or "Dear Sirs" neglects the woman, and you know the fury of a woman scorned. Especially if you're asking for money. I checked with *Ms* magazine, which suggested "Dear Gentlepeople," or "Dear Gentlepersons," but that seems so strained, artificial and old-fashioned that I could only write it with a quill pen. "Dear Friends" isn't right either. They certainly aren't my friends if they're not paying me, and they may even be potential enemies.

Then I recalled that we also don't have a word for "his or her." This leads to such abominable sentences as "Everybody who agrees raise his or her right hand," or to such flagrantly ungrammatical sentences as "Everybody who agrees raise their right hand." We also have no word for brothers *and* sisters together. "Siblings" isn't adequate. Would you say to your children, "All right, siblings, go out and play"?

Am I not in the right? We don't have an acceptable way of saying that either. "Ain't I?" won't do, even if the word is now listed in Webster's Third. "Aren't I?" is more disastrous, and affected into the bargain. "Amn't I?" sounds like Pennsylvania Dutch or like a person talking with an arrow through the throat. So we're stuck with "Am I not?" which sounds as prissy and as formal as Eliza Doolittle at her first tea party.

There you have it, the whole chapter I didn't write for this book. I simply didn't know enough to be a coauthor. I think I might have written the chapter on Professional Word Abusers. I've always thought that for the layman to get through to the meaning of professional people, barricaded behind their jargon, is like cutting through an acre of barbed wire. But I couldn't have done the chapter as well, or found half the examples that my daughter did.

All the other chapters are beyond me. In a lifetime of reading I have discovered very few genuinely informative books, mostly because people who know anything are too busy to write books about it. This is an informative book. More important, it is a fun book to read.

I agree with T. S. Eliot, a pretty fair country writer, that "the most heinous offense a writer can commit is dullness— all of the other vices result in lesser offenses."

So forget that you're learning something, and read this book for sheer pleasure. I'll make a deal with you. I'll read it over again too, starting now, and I'll try to forget that my daughter knows more than I do.

1

Cries and Calls

Words are the legs of the mind; they bear it about, carry it from point to point, bed it down at night and keep it off the ground and out of marsh and mists.

Richard Eder

One fine Tuesday in May in the year 40,000 B.C., Ak the caveman was out picking berries for the fresh fruit cup his wife was planning for dinner. Suddenly, he heard a rustling in the undergrowth. He stopped chewing and listened intently—rustlings in the undergrowth were nothing to sniff at in 40,000 B.C., what with all the animalia carnivora prowling around, looking for an Ak to grind.

A moment later, Ak saw a saber-toothed tiger stroll casually out of the undergrowth about twenty feet in front of him. Instinctively, Ak put his hand to his mouth to give the cry of danger and alert the tribe. Then he had a thought. If he *did* cry out, he might call the tiger's attention to him. Now, a saber-toothed tiger's attention is definitely something to be avoided when one is alone and armed only with a bowl of blueberries. So Ak kept quiet, and the tiger, which was upwind of him, moved to the other side of the clearing and disappeared. Ak raced home to the cave, where his wife saw that he didn't have the berries she had sent him to get—she should never have trusted a man to do her shopping—and started to make very loud noises indicating displeasure. The other members of the tribe, unaware of Ak's agitation, listened with amusement.

And then a remarkable thing happened. In a flash of inspiration, Ak turned to the other members of his tribe and uttered the cry of danger. The men looked around, alarmed, and saw nothing. They looked at Ak, puzzled. Ak gave the call of danger again. The group studied him intently—had the strain of cave life gotten to be too much for him? In a last attempt to communicate, Ak uttered the cry a third time and pointed to the entrance to the cave. This time the others understood: the cry didn't mean that there was any present danger; it meant Ak had encountered something dangerous sometime before and in a different place. The men promptly got their spears, while Ak's wife hugged him warmly to let him know she wasn't sore anymore about the berries. Then Ak and his fellow tribesmen went off to hunt the tiger.

What happened that momentous Tuesday in 40,000 B.C. between Ak and his tribe was the important first step that set man's language apart from that of the animals, and ultimately made it possible for him to conquer the world. Until that moment, man's language was hardly any different from that of the other creatures who shared his world, only a series of cries and calls used to signal an emotion or event *of the moment*. Birds use such cries and calls to signal that rain is coming, or that one bird is interested in establishing a "meaningful relationship" with another bird. In fact, most animals have fairly elaborate systems of communication through cries and calls. Dogs bark at the door to be let in, or growl threateningly if you try to take away their bone. Cats purr with pleasure when stroked, and rabbits thump the ground with their hind feet to warn their fellows to take hiding.

If man had never improved upon this primitive system of cries and calls, he would be today very much like other animals. As Susanne Langer says:

He would not talk, but grunt and gesticulate and point. He would make his wishes known, give warnings, perhaps develop a social system like that of the bees and ants, with such wonderful efficiency of communal enterprise that all men would have plenty to eat, warm apartments—all exactly alike and perfectly convenient—to live in, and everybody could and would sit in the sun or by the fire, as the climate demanded, not talking but just basking, with every want satisfied, most of his life. The young would romp and make love, the old would sleep, the middle-aged would do the routine work almost unconsciously and eat a good deal. But that would be the life of a social, superintelligent, purely sign-using animal.[1]

When Ak abstracted that cry of danger and used it apart from the *immediate* situation, it was the beginning of human language—a language consisting mostly of symbols, not signs. A symbol differs from a sign in that it is not an announcement of a condition or event that is there *right at that moment*, but merely a way of bringing a condition or event or person to mind. If you are at a party, and someone mentions President Carter, you don't turn around and expect to see him walk into the room. Instead, you probably ask, "What about President Carter?" This is a more sophisticated thought process than any animal can achieve. Fido may respond to the word "out," grab his leash, and rush for the door when he hears you say it. But if you say, "Fido, you can go *out* tomorrow," he'll still rush for that door, collar in mouth, happily expectant. He simply cannot separate the word from the event, the sign from the experience. As Bertrand Russell once remarked, "No matter how eloquently a dog may bark, he cannot tell you that his parents were poor but honest."

The distinctive feature of human communication is the ability to use symbols, to remove language from direct experience. Some people argue that the language of the bees is similar to man's, since bees can communicate very precise and complicated information about faraway pollen sources through their "dances." But the language of the bees is limited to just that—description of the location of food sources. There is no indication that bees can communicate more complex thoughts. "Gee, I saw a wonderful-looking batch of pollen yesterday, but there were men with spray guns not far away, darn it!" is beyond a bee's capacity. So is, "I think the queen is getting rather fat, don't you?" The language of bees cannot compare with the range and sophistication of man's symbols. Nor can the American sign language used by chimpanzees (the result of a remarkable series of experiments begun by R.A. and Beatrice Gardner in 1966). While chimpanzees have been shown to be capable of mastering word-symbols and even of combining them in creative new ways (one chimp, seeing a duck for the first time, called it a "water bird"), this ability remains limited. Even after intensive training and reward, not one chimp has ever attained the language skills a four-year-old human child masters without any formal training or instruction at all.

No one really knows exactly how man's sophisticated language of symbols began, though there's no dearth of theories about what man's first words were like. One is the "bow-wow" theory, which contends that the first words were imitations of the noises of animals, because these were easily recognizable by all. It's certainly easy to see how man could use the word "bow-wow" to refer to a dog. After all, that's the exact sound a dog makes, isn't it? So what could be more natural than to associate the sound with its source? The difficulty with this theory is that while *we* hear a dog's bark as "bow-wow," the French hear it as "oua-oua." The Spanish further complicate matters by using the words "guau-guau" to represent a dog's bark; the Rumanians hear it as "ham-ham," the Russians as "vas-vas," the Italians as "bu-bu," the Turks as "hov-hov," and the Chinese as "wang-wang." It's even worse when it comes to pigs. What we hear as "oink-oink," the Russians hear as "khru-khru," the Rumanians as "guits-guits," and the French as "oui-oui," which suggests that in French the pig is a cooperative beast. So the bow-wow theory really doesn't answer the important question of how humans ever came to recognize and accept *one* particular sound as a word representing a specific thing.

Obviously, the bow-wow theory has more bark than bite. Another explanation of how man arrived at his first word-sounds is called the "ding-dong" theory, which argues that all natural things give off a mystic harmonic sound all their own, a sound that man instinctively perceived and gave voice to. Again, though, the problem is that there's a wide difference in the way these "mystic" sounds, if they exist, are recorded by different languages. Even so straightforward a sound as "crash," for example, is "kling" in Danish, "krats" in Finnish, "chir-churr" in Hungarian, and "hua-la-la" in Chinese. So this theory, too, fails to explain how man came to agree that certain sounds would represent specific things.

Then there's the "yo-heave-ho" theory, which says that man's first words developed from the grunts and groans he made while doing strenuous physical labor. This theory is certainly plausible, though it still doesn't explain how man ever came to agree on what a sound would mean. We do know that the process certainly works in reverse. Words are reduced to the sounds of grunts and groans when used in the course of strenuous physical labor. Take the chant of the circus roustabouts when erecting the big tent: "Ah, heebie, hebby, hoddy, hole, go-long." An interesting sublanguage, you might think, with its own catchy rhythm. Actually, these sounds represent words, whose meaning has long since eroded: "Ah, heave it, heavy, hard, hold, go along."

One charming theory advanced by a seventeenth-century Swedish philosopher proposed that man was given his language by God, and that in the Garden of Eden, Adam and Eve spoke Danish; the Serpent, French; and God—naturally—spoke Swedish. Which gives us a neat explanation for original sin—just another "breakdown in communication."

In the end, we don't really know what man's first language was like, nor how he arrived at it . As philologist C. H. Grandgent says, "How language originated nobody knows and everybody has told." The search for the "original" language has led, in the past, to some bizarre ideas, such as the "Royal Experiment," so-called because all the experimenters were kings. The first king to try the experiment was Psammetichos, an Egyptian pharaoh. He got the notion of raising babies together in complete silence away from all other people. He thought the language these babies would speak when they finally started to talk would then be the "original" language of mankind. After a few years, when the children were brought to him, Psammetichos thought he heard one of them say the word *békos*, which is Phrygian for bread. This was sufficient proof for the pharaoh to proclaim that Phrygian was the first human language.

Later, Holy Roman Emperor Frederick II tried to repeat the Royal Experiment; it failed because the infants inconsiderately died before they were old enough to say anything. The last man to try the Royal Experiment was James IV of Scotland, who declared his venture a success when he said the children came to speak "very good Hebrew." Today we know that King James must have been fibbing to save face, because no child can learn to speak unless he hears other people speaking. Nor is any existing tongue the original language of mankind. Even the most primitive tribes existing today have languages fully as complex and sophisticated as our own. The famed linguist Edward Sapir has said that when it comes to language, "Plato walks with the Macedonian swineherd, Confucius with the head-hunting savage of Assam."

While we can't be sure what the first language was like, we are pretty sure that, like the animals, man began by using cries and calls as signals and that his ability to use words as symbols evolved much later on. His word-symbols placed him forever beyond the simple pleasure and pain of immediate experience, and helped him conceive of things and ideas he had never known. With word-symbols, man could remember and transmit the ideas of his parents, and his parents' parents, until these ideas became part of the collective memory of mankind, on which future generations could continue to build. It is not too much to say that words made civilization possible.

The difference between the simple cries and calls of animals and man's use of symbols is eloquently expressed in Helen Keller's autobiography. Here is how she describes the magical day she learned such things as words existed:

> She [her teacher, Annie Sullivan] brought me my hat, and I knew I was going out into the warm sunshine. This thought, if a wordless sensation may be called a thought, made me hop and skip with pleasure. We walked down the path to the well-house, attracted by the fragrance of the honeysuckle with which it was covered. Someone was drawing water and my teacher placed my hand under the spout. As the cool stream gushed over my hand, she spelled into the other the word "water," first slowly, then rapidly. I stood still, my whole attention fixed upon the motion of her fingers. Suddenly I felt a misty consciousness as of something forgotten—a thrill of returning thought; and somehow the mystery of language was revealed to me. I knew then that w-a-t-e-r meant the wonderful cool something that was flowing over my hand. That living word awakened my soul, gave it light, hope, set it free! I left the well-house eager to learn. Everything had a name, and each name gave birth to a new thought. As we returned to the house, every object which I touched seemed to quiver with life. That was because I saw everything with the strange, new sight that had come to me.[2]

Notice that even before Helen Keller knew about words,

she was capable of communication. When her teacher gave her a hat, she knew it meant she was going outside. But any intelligent animal, a dog, cat, or even seal can be trained to understand that. What an animal could never understand is what Helen Keller learned that fateful day, the day she became a full *human* being. She learned that the word w-a-t-e-r was not necessarily a sign that water was wanted or expected, but a way to talk about, conceive, remember the thing that is water. One simple thing sets man's language apart from the cries and calls of animals: the ability to use words apart from direct experience.

There is a danger, however, in a language of symbols, for once words become removed from things, they begin to shape their own reality. John Kenneth Galbraith calls this phenomenon "wordfact." An excellent illustration is the story of the Emperor's New Clothes. All of us know this tale of the unfortunate emperor, deceived by two dishonest tailors into believing that he was dressed in richly appointed robes when he was, in fact, naked. He looked in the mirror and saw himself undressed, but the tailors oohed and aahed and told him he was magnificently arrayed. Faced with a discrepancy between what he saw and what he was told, he decided it was his eyes that must be wrong, and believed what his tailors said. Eventually, the entire town believed the story told by the dishonest tailors and accepted the image transmitted by words over the image perceived by their eyes. *That* is wordfact.

In a movie some years ago, Joey Bishop played the role of a husband surprised by his wife while in bed with another woman. The wife enters, is horrified at the scene before her eyes, and screams at him, "How *could* you?!" Joey instantly leaps out of bed and starts getting dressed, asking innocently, "How could I what?"

"How could you have that woman in our bed?"

"What woman?" Joey asks. By this time the woman gets out of bed and is hurriedly dressing.

"Why, the woman right there, right there on the bed next to
you!!"

"There is no woman in this bed," Joey replies.

The dialogue continues until the woman is dressed and
leaves the house. At the end, confronted with a fully dressed
Joey and no sign of another woman, his wife is obliged to accept his version of what happened—there never *was* a woman
in bed with him at all. That is a triumph for wordfact.

James Fenimore Cooper, author of *The Last of the Mohi-
cans, The Pathfinder,* and *The Deerslayer,* created in his novels an American frontier that never existed—an imaginary
West that he made real for his millions of readers with such
distortions and inaccuracies that they constitute wordfact—
but many people still accept his version as real. Mark Twain,
who believed that words should bear a close relation to reality
and not become a substitute for it, mocked a typical Cooper
description of an Indian attack on a boat in his hilarious essay
"Fenimore Cooper's Literary Offenses."

> Cooper seldom saw anything correctly. He saw
> nearly all things as through a glass eye, dark-
> ly. . . . In the *Deerslayer* tale, Cooper has a stream
> which is fifty feet wide where it flows out of a lake; it
> presently narrows to twenty as it meanders along for
> no given reason, and yet when a stream acts like that it
> ought to be required to explain itself. . . . The
> stream has bends in it, a sure indication that it has al-
> luvial banks and cuts in them; yet these bends are only
> thirty and fifty feet long. If Cooper had been a nice and
> punctilious observer, he would have noticed that the
> bends were oftener nine hundred feet long than short
> of it.
>
> Cooper made the exit of that stream fifty feet wide,
> in the first place, for no particular reason; in the sec-
> ond place, he narrowed it to less than twenty to
> accommodate some Indians. He bends a "sapling" to

the form of an arch over this narrow passage, and conceals six Indians in its foliage. They are "laying" for a settler's scow or ark which is coming up the stream on its way to the lake; it is being hauled against the stiff current by a rope whose stationary end is anchored in the lake; its rate of progress cannot be more than a mile an hour. Cooper describes the ark, but pretty obscurely. In the matter of dimensions, "it was little more than a canal-boat." Let us guess, then, that it was about one hundred and forty feet long. It was of "greater breadth than common." Let us guess, then, that it was about sixteen feet wide. This leviathan had been prowling down bends which were but a third as long as itself, and scraping between banks where it had only two feet of space to spare on each side. We cannot too much admire this miracle. A low-roofed log dwelling occupies "two thirds of the ark's length," a dwelling ninety feet long and sixteen feet wide, let us say. . . . The ark is arriving at the stream's exit now, whose width has been reduced to less than twenty feet to accommodate the Indians—say to eighteen. There is a foot to spare on either side of the boat. Did the Indians notice that there was going to be a tight squeeze there? Did they notice that they could make money by climbing down out of that arched sapling and just stepping aboard when the ark scraped by? No, other Indians would have noticed these things, but Cooper's Indians never notice anything.

The ark is one hundred and forty feet long; the dwelling is ninety feet long. The idea of the Indians is to drop softly and secretly from the arched sapling to the dwelling as the ark creeps along under it at the rate of one mile an hour, and butcher the family. It will take the ark a minute and a half to pass under. It will take the ninety-foot dwelling a minute to pass under. Now, then, what did the six Indians do? It would take you thirty years to guess, and even then you would have to give it up, I believe. Therefore, I will tell you what the Indians did. Their chief, a person of quite extraordinary intellect for a Cooper Indian, warily watched the canal-boat as it squeezed along under him, and when he had got his calculations fined down to exactly the right shade, as he judged, he let go and dropped. And *missed the house!* That is actually what he did. He missed the house, and landed in the stern of the scow. It was not much of a fall, yet it knocked him silly. . . .

There still remained in the roost five Indians. Let me explain what the five did—you would not be able to reason it out for yourself. No. 1 jumped for the boat, but fell in the water astern of it. Then No. 2 jumped for the boat, but fell in the water still farther astern of it. Then No. 3 jumped for the boat, and fell a good way astern of it. Then No. 4 jumped for the boat and fell in the water *away* astern. Then even No. 5 made a jump for the boat—for he was a Cooper Indian. In the matter of intellect, the difference between a Cooper Indian and the Indian that stands in front of the cigar-shop is not spacious. . . . [3]

Of course, Cooper's books are works of fiction, and he's entitled to a degree of invention. But millions of readers still accept Cooper's West That Never Was as the real thing. And that is another triumph for wordfact.

Not all examples are amusing. Karl Menninger, an eminent psychiatrist, has argued that in some cases, wordfact can even be fatal. The very word "cancer," he says, "may well kill some patients who would not have succumbed [so quickly] to the malignancy from which they suffer." African witch doctors have long been aware of the power of wordfact, and many otherwise healthy men and women have sickened and died because of the power of their belief in the witch doctor's curse. There can be no better example of the word become fact.

Some people believe that wordfact is also often behind the diagnosis of psychiatric disturbances. Once someone is labeled as "paranoid" or "manic-depressive" or "schizophren-ic," it is practically impossible to be reclassified—even if the diagnosis is wrong—because people are so dependent on wordfact they accept the classification over the observable fact. This is chillingly demonstrated in *Titicut Follies*, a docu-mentary movie filmed in a mental institution. The film is so graphic and the things it reveals about the treatment of mental patients so disturbing, that it was shown only over the strenu-ous objections of the Massachusetts legislature. In one scene, a patient (who appears very rational) asks the doctor (whose nervous tics and wild eyes make him seem like a borderline mental case himself), "What makes me insane and you sane? What's the difference in the way we think and function?" The doctor's answer: "You are in here; I am not. You are a pa-tient; I am not." In other words, it's the word "patient" that makes the man insane. Anyone defined as a "psychotic" must be "crazy." As Polonius says to Queen Gertrude in Act II, Scene II, of *Hamlet*, "Your noble son is mad:/Mad call I it; for, to define true madness,/What is 't but to be nothing else but mad?"

Many old and familiar traditions are based on nothing more than wordfact. Our calendar, for example. There's no natural law of the universe that decrees one day shall be Friday and the next Saturday; August 26 is only August 26 because we *say* it is. But by now, the names of the days are so familiar that to most of us it seems as if to change them would be to change the nature of time itself. In 1752, the British govern-ment decided to adjust the calendar so it would reflect as-tronomical reality more closely. To accomplish this, it was an-nounced that September 2 would become September 14 that year, and all the days between would simply be skipped over. The British people were in an uproar over this decree; letters poured into Parliament protesting that the change was an out-rage, since it would deprive everyone of twelve days of his life!

The prize for wordfact calendar reform, however, goes to the Prague government, which recently released this edict:

> Because Christmas Eve will fall on a Thursday, that day will be considered a Saturday for work purposes. Factories will be closed all day, although stores will remain open a half day only. Friday, December 25, will be considered a Sunday, with both factories and stores open all day. Monday, December 28, will be a Wednesday for work purposes. Wednesday will be a business Friday. Saturday will be a Sunday, and Sunday will be a Monday.

That's a reconstruction of reality through language that sounds positively Orwellian.

It was, indeed, George Orwell who predicted that, by 1984, wordfact would reign supreme, and people would believe such dictates as "War is peace" and "Ignorance is strength." We may be arriving at that point even sooner than Orwell thought. When Indira Gandhi was Prime Minister of India she contended that she had jailed political opponents and silenced all opposition in India "in the interest of preserving democracy." It was also "in the interest of preserving democracy" that the Shah of Iran recently established military rule in his country. And Yasir Arafat has stated that his terrorist army, the PLO, does "not want to destroy any people," adding, "It is precisely because we have been advocating coexistence that we have shed so much blood." This calls to mind the similar statement by a U.S. Army lieutenant during the Vietnam War: "We had to destroy the village in order to save it." During an interview with David Frost, Richard Nixon said that unconstitutional actions by the President were justified "if undertaken for the purpose of preserving the Constitution." He later added that while the President was not "above the law," he could break the law when necessary. Nixon was a master of wordfact.

History itself is continually being rewritten by wordfact. The American Bicentennial was responsible for a patriotic outpouring that led to some interesting reinterpretations of the American Revolution. Commenting on George Washington's defeat at White Plains, New York, on October 28, 1776, the cochairman of the Bicentennial Committee of the City of White Plains said, "Yes, we got thrown off the hill, but we stood our ground." And describing Lafayette's humiliating rout by British troops at Conshohocken, Pennsylvania, a colonel of the Bicentennial Commission of Pennsylvania said proudly, "That was a tactical withdrawal. They did a lot of that during the Revolution."

Recently, Alvaro Cunhal, secretary general of the Portuguese Communist party, provided a striking illustration of wordfact. "We think, yes, that the Soviet Union is a democratic country. It is one of the countries where there is one of the most ample democracies," Cunhal said. Fair enough, if he really believes that. But when this same Mr. Cunhal states that "We Communists don't accept the rules of the election game," adding immediately that in Portugal "if there is one party that has been for democracy, it is the Communist party," one is entitled to wonder if words have any real meaning except as hortatory emotional signals.

When words are continually twisted and wrenched to create wordfact, they eventually come to mean nothing at all. Hemingway deplored the way that the words "sacred" and "honor" have been drained of meaning through overuse. After all, if every cause is "sacred" and every man "honorable," then no cause is sacred and no man honorable. As Adamov said about words used loosely to talk about things that never were and never would be: "Worn, threadbare, filed down, (these) words have become the carcass of words, phantom words; everyone drearily chews and regurgitates the sound of them between their jaws."

2

Professional Word Abusers

Who is this that darkeneth counsel by words without knowledge?

Job 38:2

Some time ago, my husband and I decided to buy a life insurance policy. When the policy arrived in the mail, in fine print on the reverse side of the paper, I read the following statement:

> Any receipt for payment made is subject to the condition that it shall be void if any check or draft, to whomsoever payable, taken for or on account of the amount specified herein is dishonored for any reason and that no such check or draft shall constitute a payment to the Company, whether or not the amount due, or any part thereof, has been advanced or credited to the Company by any of its representatives, and that any check or draft so taken may be handled in accordance with the practice of any collecting bank.

I really don't know what that sentence means. I think it means that it's not *nice* to fool the John Hancock Insurance Company, but I can't be sure. And this linguistic monstrosity is just one small proof that in the art of pumping air into the language, the legal profession can hold its own with anyone.

Imagine the following movie scenario: It is a desert at high noon. The sun beats down relentlessly on the dry sands. The temperature is 110 degrees in the shade—and there is no shade. Even the cacti wilt in this, God's merciless oven. Suddenly, over the horizon, a figure appears. The camera zooms in, and we see a man, crawling along on his hands and knees, head up, one leg dragging—you know, the way he does just before he cries out, "Water! Water!"? He is the foreman of a nearby ranch, whose horse and water were stolen from him by a heartless highwayman. Then, a breakaway shot to the right, where we see another black dot on the horizon. Again the camera zooms in, and we see a man in pitiful condition, fevered, broken, bloody, and near death. He is a lawyer.

Slowly, the men inch nearer each other. At last they meet. The lawyer, realizing that he is about to die from multiple wounds inflicted by a client who went berserk when he read the deed the lawyer had drawn up, decides, in a final moment of kindness, to give the foreman the last few drops left in his water flask. Being a lawyer, however, he doesn't just reach into his sack, pull out the flask, and say, "Here, have a drink on me." Even in the final throes of his death agony, no lawyer who has ever passed a bar examination would dream of saying something as simple as, "Have a drink." With the determination bred of years of training and practice in the fine art of gobbledygook, our lawyer summons all his strength to say,

> I (hereinafter referred to as the donor) hereby donate, bequeath, and relinquish to you (hereinafter known as the donee) all appurtenant rights and advantages deriving from the use, enjoyment, and possession of said flask, including, but not limited to, all coverings, carrying straps, and water contained therein, this covenant to be binding notwithstanding any other document or documents, deed or deeds, of whatever nature or kind whatsoever, to the contrary.

By this time, unfortunately, the foreman has expired, so our lawyer has to go to the trouble of revising his statement to include any children, or issue, of the foreman, as beneficiaries of his water flask. Can we hope that before he is able to finish, he, too, will pass on to final judgment by the Heavenly Barrister? No, worse luck, he is rescued at the last moment by a circuit court judge and so will live on to confound, confuse, and aggravate untold thousands of his fellowmen with the insane redundancies and indirectness of legalese.

You may think that this is just a fabrication, an outrageous exaggeration of the language of the law. The real thing is often no less absurd. A county attorney recently submitted this letter to the hearing officer in a grievance suit:

> Pursuant to subsection 204.12 of the Rules of PERB, Onondaga Community College respectfully requests both an extension of the time to file exceptions to the findings and order of the Hearing Officer and an extension of the time to file said exceptions.

Which makes the entire matter about as clear as marsh mud.

How about this gem, which arrived after a friend of ours had received some merchandise in the mail: "It is hereby stipulated and agreed by the undersigned, jointly and severally, that all payments due and owing to the party of the first part may be remitted to the party of the second part on or before and not later than a period of 14 days subsequent to the receipt of the notice hereinto included." Would you believe that what is being said here is, "You can pay in two weeks"? Can anyone be blamed for not knowing that "voucherable expenditures may be incurred" really means "you can charge it"?

Most lawyers seem to have sworn fealty to a Hyperfustian Code, whereby they agree that whenever they are given a choice between two forms of a word, a long one and a short one, they will take the long one. How else can one explain a linguistic barbarism like "summarization" (part of a scheme to warm up the North Pole?) when what is really meant is "summary"? Or the use of "origination" for "origin" (remember Darwin's great book, *On the Origination of Species*)? Then there's "administrate" for "administer," "notate" for "note," and "orientate" for "orient." One can't help wondering if men who write like this are able to decompress when talking at home:

"Hello, dear." (Gives wife a kiss.) "That's to confirmate arrival at destination." ("I'm home.")
"Good, dear. Wash up; there's pot roast for dinner tonight."
"Pot roast? Again? Let me avail myself of this opportunity to registrate the extent of my displeasure and notate that a possible dénouement is a case of expectorization by the party of the first part." ("I'm so mad I could just spit.")

Of course, most legal forms are not meant to be read by anyone other than a lawyer, similarly trained in the art of obfuscation, and some of the jargon may be necessary to make gossamer distinctions in law. Often the language employed is meant to be a bulwark against any conceivable legal action—and therefore is made so painfully explicit and detailed that there can be no possible room for other interpretation. Convoluted legal forms exist so that someday the company lawyer can say, "No, you can't sue us for that; it says quite clearly in paragraph 4, subdivision b, section 1, that this agreement is in effect *unless* and *until* etc., etc." True legalese is really prefabricated argument, created to stave off an assault before one is even contemplated.

Still, most legal tautologies and long forms are unnecessary. David Mellinkoff, an attorney, says that, "There is little legal prose of any sort which cannot be made more intelligible than it usually is." Apparently, the New York State Legislature agrees, since it recently passed a bill outlawing unintelligible legal jargon. Loan agreements, apartment leases, and other consumer contracts will now have to be written in "non-technical language" using "words with common and everyday meanings." Businesses that do not comply are liable to class action suits of up to $10,000. Citibank in New York was one of the first to work out a simplified version of its loan form in compliance with the new law. A comparison of the old and new contracts shows the dramatic improvement:

Old Form	New Form
For value received, the undersigned (jointly and severally) hereby promise to pay . . . the sum of ———.	To repay my loan, I promise to pay you ———dollars.
In the event of default in the payment of this or any other obligation, or the performance or observance of any term or covenant contained herein . . . or the bank shall deem itself insecure . . . the bank shall have the right at its option without demand or notice of any kind, to declare . . . the obligations to be immediately due and payable.	I'll be in default: 1. If I don't pay an installment on time, or 2. If any other creditor tries by legal process to take any money of mine in your possession. You can then demand immediate payment of the balance of this note.

Unfortunately, even before the law went into effect, it was vigorously attacked by infuriated lawyers who argued that "plain talk" in legal contracts is vague and dangerously ambiguous. An odd argument when one considers how ambiguous the existing legal forms are. Mellinkoff describes legalese as an "art of planned confusion" in which deliberate ambiguity protects lawyers from ever having to take responsibility for an unwise course of action.

Take, for example, the "one-legged subjunctive," a favorite trick that helps lawyers plant both their feet firmly in midair. The one-legged subjunctive usually appears in the form "it would seem," as in "it would seem that one of the out-comes of this course of action is that expenditures may be in-curred exceeding the limits of . . . " etc. There's a magnifi-cent mistiness surrounding the one-legged subjunctive. "It would seem," says the lawyer—and leaves you hanging there, waiting for the completion of his thought. But we never do get to the other half, the implied "but the fact is" or "but this is not the case." Just "it would seem"—and that's all. Now if things don't develop the way he expected, the lawyer can hardly be called to account for it. After all, he didn't say that was the way things *were*, just that at the time that's the way things *seemed* to be. He has managed not to commit himself to any definite opinion or course of action. It is very hard to hold a man accountable for what he is saying if he is not saying anything.

Government officials are among the worst abusers of the language. They use language for wilier purposes than mere muddling. Bureaucratese helps to create an impression of or-der and stability, and of a condition where everything is under sure control. If circumstances should happen to contradict a government official, then he simply pumps more hot air into the language and floats it away from the disagreeable facts. Press Secretary Ron Ziegler's now classic remark that one of President Nixon's obviously mendacious statements was "no longer operative" is an excellent example. How apparently reasonable that sounds. A statement that was once operative just *isn't* anymore, so the question of its truth or falsehood ceases to exist. No muss, no fuss, nothing for us to get all concerned about. After all, one can hardly blame a man if his statement breaks down, any more than we would blame him if his car broke down. There's also the suggestion here that somehow the statement can now be taken in for repairs and fixed. If Ron Ziegler had been around to write press releases for other celebrated figures of the past, we might now have on record such disclaimers as these, invented by journalist Sid-ney Harris:

Jack the Ripper: I regret that my sexual anomalies, stemming from a repression in childhood, led me to indiscreet violation of the persons of some ladies.

John Dillinger: Within the time frame of my youth, it was my proclivity toward derring-do that led to further acts of doubtful legitimacy.

Attila the Hun: Perhaps it was excessive zeal, but I sincerely felt that the welfare of Western barbarism made it imperative to halt the spread of civilization by any means within my power.

Judas Iscariot: In extenuation, may I remind you that the man was a troublemaker, an outside agitator from Nazareth, and obviously trying to subvert law and order.[1]

If you want to appear in control and on top of things, then you can never admit that you don't know the answer to something. I cannot resist the temptation to quote Ron Ziegler one more time; he is, as Winston Churchill said of Ramsay Mac-Donald, "a man with the gift of compressing the largest amount of words into the smallest amount of thoughts." Here, Ziegler is answering a question about the condition of some of the Watergate tapes:

I would feel that most of the conversations that took place in those areas of the White House that did have the recording system would in almost their entirety be in existence but the special prosecutor, the court, and I think, the American people are sufficiently familiar with the recording system to know where the recording devices existed and to know the situation in terms of the recording process but I feel, although the process has not been undertaken yet in preparation of the material to abide by the court decision, really, what the answer to that question is.

The sheer bulk of words suggests that something is being

said. If you look at the statement closely, however, you see that Ziegler is simply saying, "I don't know."

This same desire to make problems seem stable and under control must have been behind then-Vice-President Rockefeller's comment that the reason the national economy was in such a mess was that the Administration had not yet been able to "conceptualize a solution." That's much more reassuring than hearing the President doesn't have the foggiest idea of what to do next, isn't it? Or listen to Alan Greenspan, former Chairman of the President's Council of Economic Advisers, explain why inflation wasn't going away:

> It is a very tricky policy problem to find the particular calibration and timing that would be appropriate to stem the acceleration in risk premiums created by falling incomes without prematurely aborting the decline in the inflation-generated risk premiums.

The power to obscure the flame of meaning in the smoke of words did not disappear with the Nixon Administration. There is ample evidence that the talent has survived into the Jimmy Carter era. Less than a week after Carter commanded that all government documents be written in language "as clear and simple as possible," he signed into law an order for a tariff increase on imported citizen-band radios which included the following statement:

> Expedited adjustment assistance would be ineffective in helping the industry cope with current problems of severe inventory overhang, low prices, and financial losses.

In plain English, this appears to mean that federal aid to American manufacturers of citizen-band radios will not help solve their financial problems.

Here is Secretary of the Treasury W. Michael Blumenthal offering cryptic comfort to the Italian government of Premier Giulio Andreotti:

I was pleased to learn that during the coming year the Government plans to attack the twin problems of inflation and external disequilibrium, while aiming for a rate of growth which will not exacerbate other domestic economic problems.

This same kind of verbal posturing is found in a government spokesman's recent reference to "advance downward adjustments"—in other words, budget cuts. Another official used the term "confrontation management" when what he really meant was "riot control."

Officialese is sometimes used to cover up the most tragic errors. Reporting on the Teton Dome collapse in Idaho that killed fourteen people, the investigating panel concluded that the calamity was due to "an unfortunate choice of design measures together with less than conventional precautions." *The New York Times* of June 26, 1977, included this report of a fatal fire:

Cyanide fumes and carbon monoxide pouring from a padded cell apparently set afire by a juvenile inmate were said to have caused the deaths of 42 inmates and visitors at Maury County jail in Columbia, Tenn., Sunday. The gases were generated by the fire in the padding. On the basis of tests, the padding was said to be nonflammable, but those tests "may not have been appropriate," one official said.

What exactly did this official mean? Your guess is as appropriate as mine.

In "The Briefing," Peter Berger imagines how a government spokesman, by the adroit use of language, maintains this posture of "steady at the controls" in the face of the ultimate crisis:

Q. Last night a flaming red sky in the North could be seen from every port of the United States. Also last night, millions of Americans saw on all three networks

the mile high figure of an angel with a sword in his right hand. Do you feel that the term "alleged apparition" is still the proper language for this?
A. I'm not authorized to change the language of the announcement.
Q. Is the White House aware of the possibility that the apparition may spell the end of the world?
A. It seems to me that the use of alarmist language is counter-productive.[2]

In bureaucratese, the use of big words gives the simplest ideas the appearance of being major pronouncements. Gerald Ford was recently a guest lecturer at Yale, where he was asked which former President he likes best. His answer? "I identify affirmatively with Harry Truman."

Words like routinization, credibility, time frame, delivery systems, input, downplay, and prioritize help government spokesmen appear knowledgeable while actually saying little. About twelve years ago, the publishers of *The American Heritage Dictionary of the English Language* gathered a group of well-known critics and authors to serve as a "Usage Panel" to pass judgment on new language coinages. Government bureaucratese, expectedly, did not fare well. Here are some of the panel's comments:

On the use of "downplay" (as in "the delegate downplayed the reported anxiety over the party's abortion plank"):

Robert Coughlan: Revolting.

Jacques Barzun: What's wrong with "played down"? Shall we be saying "The defeated candidate ingave"?

Peter De Vries: If I heard a speaker use it, I would up-get and outwalk.

On "input": (as in "The President had access to varied input"):

Nat Hentoff: Mechanical shorthand that rusts thought.

* * *

Jacques Barzun: . . . jargon—and very vague, since input can mean anything from a Congressional appropriation to a frankfurter at lunch.

Lewis Mumford: It is the equivalent of "y'know" for those who don't know the right word.

Peter De Vries: The thought of putting information into a President is a little grotesque.

On "prioritize" (as in "a first attempt to prioritize the tasks facing the new administration"):

Heywood Hale Broun: I'm afraid this one head-acheizes me too much for sensible comment.

Russell Baker: Pentagonese. Are we all going to start writing like a building?

In a devastating indictment of government officialese, Stuart Chase cites the following instance:

A New York plumber wrote the Bureau of Standards in Washington that he had found hydrochloric acid fine for cleaning drains, and was it harmless? Washington replied: "The efficacy of hydrochloric acid is indisputable, but the chlorine residue is incompatible with metallic permanence."

The plumber wrote back that he was mighty glad the bureau agreed with him. The bureau replied with a note of alarm: "We cannot assume responsibility for the production of toxic and noxious residues with hydrochloric acid, and suggest that you use an alternate procedure." The plumber was happy to learn that the bureau still agreed with him.

Whereupon Washington exploded: "Don't use hydrochloric acid; it eats the hell out of the pipes!"[3]

Government lawyers and bureaucrats are not the only ones guilty of pumping air into a language that every year threatens to balloon away from us. More and more professions are developing specialized vocabularies that often serve no other purpose than to increase the member's feeling of importance and exclude the layman. "Every profession has its growing arsenal of jargon to fire at the layman and hurl him back from its walls," says journalist William Zinsser. Nor is science, that supposedly precise art, innocent of this kind of word abuse. Consider words like infrastructure, functionalism, gradualism, time-phase, systematized, and organizational— all designed to make simple ideas seem complex. A glance at any recent scientific journal yields abundant examples of scientese:

> Uncouplers are molecules with protonophoric and ionophoric capabilities that mediate coupled cyclical transport of cations, forming cation-containing complexes with electrogenic ionophores that potentiate cyclical transport of cations.

In scientese, it is absolutely forbidden to come right out and state an idea; no, you must walk around it first, consider how it is dressed and how it will look in your living room, and the kind of day it was when you first saw it. Then you must go over to inspect its neighbors and relatives and friends and inquire as to their health, and when you are done with that, you stroll over to the family vaults to check out its parentage. *Then* and only then you come out and say, "This is my idea; this is what I think."

The simplest and most familiar homilies are rendered incomprehensible when translated into scientese:

> One of the remarkable and characteristic properties currently under intensive laboratory study is that when a metallic receptacle is subjected to a careful and continuous scrutiny of a deliberate nature, the mixture which it is the nature and purpose of the said receptacle to contain will not, in point of fact, undergo a phase change and permit entry into a gaseous form at any point in time within the duration of the aforementioned scrutiny.

In other words, a watched pot never boils.

> We have found that the individual under study should find the most feasible means that will enable him or her, as the case may be, to enter into a rapid repose, facilitating, as soon as possible, an actual somnolent condition along an interface as well as a precocious cessation of the condition and re-entry into a scheduled plan of activities that will maximize salubrious and/or salutary conditions, in addition to factors which favor a rise in profits or, as the circumstances may dictate, greater growth in the level of mental performance and achievement.

In other words: Early to bed and early to rise makes a man healthy, wealthy, and wise.

Some scientists defend the use of gobbledygook, claiming that their language is complicated because the ideas are complicated, and if they were to translate the ideas into simpler language, the meaning would be lost. There is a difference, they contend, between obscurity of expression and the expression of obscurity. They point out that a Disney cartoon once explained a nuclear chain reaction by showing a large floor covered with mousetraps loaded with Ping-Pong balls. When another ball was thrown at the floor, the traps began to go off in an accelerating sequence until it seemed that all the Ping-Pong balls were bouncing at once. Although the public can grasp this idea easily, say the science writers, it is an inaccurate representation of what a nuclear reaction is *really* like.

Fair enough. But then how do you account for the fact that Einstein and Newton, whose concepts were the most advanced of their day, explained their ideas in plain, straightforward language? And how do you explain the fact that gobbledygook carries over from scientists' writing into their everyday speech? A professor of biochemistry at Boston University gave a Christmas party and thoughtfully went to the trouble of photocopying directions to his house. The direc-

tions began with, "My house is physically located on . . . "
There's a perfect example of what linguists (who have their
own hang-ups with big words) would call a pleonasm—a useless word, a superabundance of parts. How else could his
house be located? Spiritually? Emotionally? Whatever happened to good old "My house is on . . . "?

A mind trained in the intricacies of scientese will use it in all
situations. In a laudable attempt to improve the quality of
teaching at New York's Upstate Medical Center, the faculty
began polling the students for their opinions of the professors
teaching the biochemistry course for medical students. The
students were given forms on which they could rate the
professors (to make sure of an honest response, the students
did not give their names), and the results of the evaluations
were given to each professor privately. A fine idea—not at all
complicated. Here is how it is described on the print-out
sheet:

> Previous opinion poll analyses from our students had
> revealed that our students give reliable opinions of
> faculty teaching with regard to three relatively inde-
> pendent factors. With these results in mind a 45-state-
> ment experimental instrument was devised containing
> 15 statements pertaining to each of these three fac-
> tors. . . .
>
> This form allows a quick summary of the data to be
> obtained for each factor and is presented in the form
> of 1) a histogram of median values (the x's) and 2) per-
> centaile and median values of medians.

Lest you were disturbed by the complexity of that, the writer hastens to point out that "such a summary is not without its
problems" and adds an important footnote: "Equal weight
for each statement as it applies to the factor is assumed; this is
actually inaccurate."

All clear, everyone?

The excuse that unreadably abstruse language is necessary

because scientific ideas are so complex doesn't hold water (or should I say that it will not encompass a measurable quantity of a potable mixture of hydrogen and oxygen not in a gaseous or solid state). The language is not complicated because the ideas are complicated, but because the mind of the author is so hopelessly sunk in gobbledygook that it has drowned in the stuff.

There are many reasons why scientists choose to communicate in this way. For one, scientists, like lawyers and government officials, are generally unwilling to go out on a limb. Or rather, they are unwilling to go out on a limb accompanied by nothing but a simple declarative sentence. This is why they write such circuitously long sentences, to include all the qualifications and modifications—the "ifs" and "unlesses" and "in the case ofs" that keep them safely within reach of the main trunk—just in case that limb should start to crack:

> Notwithstanding the problems of selecting the control group and the difficulties in determining all variables, and allowing for the large standard deviations of the experimental group, these data suggest the possibility that vitamin C may have some positive value in prevention of the common cold, *if* the disease is of bacterial origin and *if* the patient refrains from ingesting mineral supplements for the duration of the vitamin C therapy.

One wonders how the man who wrote that has the courage to decide to get out of bed in the morning.

Scientists' fondness for the passive tense ("It has been found that" instead of "We found") may stem from their desire to avoid appearing "boastful." If so, that is a becoming modesty, but what if the great men of history had shared this exquisitely refined sensibility? Caesar would never have said, "I came, I saw, I conquered," but "The place was arrived at, was observed, and was duly overtaken." Paul Revere would have gone through the streets of Boston shouting, "An arrival of the British has been noted!'' (or even notated!).

No, modesty cannot be the only explanation for the scientists' passion for the passive tense. They think this use of the passive lends their papers an air of objectivity and detachment, and makes it seem as though they are unveiling universal truth rather than the results of a fallible experiment. Doesn't ''It is suggested that'' or ''It is believed that'' sound more convincing than ''I think''? A scientist always tries to avoid appearing as if he cares personally about the results of his experiments; he is, he would have it seem, interested only in the pursuit of verifiable truth, wherever that may lead. In reality, of course, he would rather lose his dog than a pet theory.

While we're on the subject of word abuse in the realm of science, let's not forget physicians. Medical jargon is among the most impenetrable and forbidding in the entire empire of verbal mystification. Much of the doctor's abstruse language may be a necessary result of specialization. A surgeon performing open heart surgery isn't likely to tell the nurse, ''Hand me that long, sharp thingummy; I'm going to join this red, rubbery job to that other one over there,'' although that might be as direct and satisfactory under the circumstances as what he does say.

Too often, however, doctors use medical jargon when they don't have to—just to impress the gullible layman. Indeed, word abuse in medical practice is a time-honored tradition dating all the way back to the thirteenth century, when the medieval physician Arnold of Villanova wrote a treatise urging his fellow doctors to fall back on impressive-sounding language when they could not diagnose a patient's disease. ''Say that he has an obstruction of the liver,'' Arnold wrote, ''and particularly use the word 'obstruction' because patients do not understand what it means.'' Back in those days, before the advent of penicillin and sulfa drugs, there was little else the doctor could impress his patients with except words. But the tradition has survived into the era of modern medicine,

and Arnold of Villanova's advice is still being honored. Today, if a doctor is unable to diagnose a patient's disease, he
may solemnly pronounce it to be G.O.K.—"God only
knows." Michael Crichton, an author who also got his M.D.
at Harvard Medical School, recently perused some back issues of the *New England Journal of Medicine.* He was ap-
palled by the "dense, impressive, and forbidding" prose.
Some examples:

> Interest and concern in health care is based to an im-
> portant extent on the viability of the biomedical re-
> search enterprise whose success in turn de-
> pends . . .

> Corticosteroids, antimalarial drugs and other agents
> may impede degranulation, because of their ability to
> prevent granule membranes from rupturing, to inhibit
> ingestion or to interfere with the degranulation mech-
> anism per se.

Of course, these examples are drawn from medical journals, and medical journals are read mostly by doctors. Can it
be that doctors are so steeped in the use of jargon that they
cannot turn it off even when among their compatriots? Michael Crichton thinks that doctors use jargon as a form of
group recognition, "rather like a secret fraternal handshake."
He adds, "It is a game, and everybody plays it. Indeed, I suspect that one refuses to play at one's professional peril."

In short, doctors speak and write medical jargon for the
same reasons that lawyers use legalese—to increase their
sense of self-importance, to impress and exclude the layman
from their exclusive club, and to give an appearance of order
and stability, where often there is none. This last reason is
certainly what is behind much of the language of space, a
comparatively recent arrival in the scientific field.

In spacetalk, you never say that something is going wrong:
you say there's an "anomaly." With seeming logic, you also

don't say if something is going right; you say it's "nominal."
(That's the big problem with our criminal justice system today; so many people just don't teach their children the difference between nominal and anomaly.) If all this isn't
enough to bring out your anomal instincts, think about the
way NASA described the return to earth of the three astronauts who linked up with the Russians. They landed, according to official reports, in "stable two" position—in other
words, upside down. The same oblique use of language led
one airline company to describe the crash of a civilian plane
as the pilot's "failure to maintain sufficient altitude to avoid
neighboring terrain." As they say in Soho, "When the plane
'its the terrain, it's the plane wot gets 'urt."

Astronaut, doctor, physicist, microbiologist—none of them
can hold a candle to that dread practitioner of scientific gobbledygook—the sociologist. Sociology is a relatively new
science concerned not with complicated mathematical equa-
tions or laws of the physical universe, but with the ordinary
affairs of ordinary people. So naturally it follows that the sociologist is able—nay, willing, even eager—to speak and write
in simple and direct language. Right? Well, a reasonable person might think so, but reason and sociology took two divergent roads way back there somewhere.

No, precisely *because* the subject matter is so easy to
grasp, the sociologist becomes more anxious to prove to the
world that he is engaged in weighty and impenetrable studies.
He does this by concocting a vocabulary almost laughable for
the way it masquerades the simplest ideas in the highest-
sounding phrases—a sheep in wolf's clothing, as it were.

In 1976, more than thirty-five hundred sociologists descend-
ed on Washington for the 71st American Sociological Association Conference. More than seven hundred papers were
presented before the convention's end, groaning under such
titles as, "A Model for Examination of Multi-Cultural
Stresses Experienced by the Latin Population in a Pluralistic
Context." The keynote speaker opened the conference with

this remark: "We are a heterogeneous population with divergent opinions on historicism, longitudinal research and theoretical orientation of symbolic interactionism." One can, of course, sympathize with the man. It would be hard to gather any group of people in a room to talk about such controversial, deeply felt matters as historicism, longitudinal research, and theoretical orientation of symbolic interactionism without the discussion becoming heated.

It doesn't take a convention of thirty-five hundred sociologists to fill the air with a cloud of confusion. A single sociologist can manage that very nicely, as was recently proven when one came to speak to me and my colleagues at Onondaga Community College, where I teach. He began his address with a lengthy and obscure discussion of man as "a meaning-making organism" and moved on to discuss the concept of "meta-feel," which turned out to be his word for "experience." We were then enlightened by his "Paradigm on Assumptions About Truth," which included such subtopics as "interpersonal context created for the learner" and "interpersonal leverage in response to resistance." In one of his moments of greater clarity, he asked earnestly, "How can we get people to *resonate* together?" One of my colleagues, disgusted with the verbal miasma, whispered, "Bounce them against each other very rapidly inside a large steel drum."

No matter how simple the idea, a sociologist can manage to complicate it. One research group that wanted to study people's response to newspaper ads in the Personal Column ran the following item in the *Singles News Register:* "Potential partners seek to strike bargains which maximize their rewards in the exchange of assets." We can thank heaven that sociologists have not yet tried to be songwriters; if they did, we might now be struggling with lyrics like, "I've Never Maximized Anyone's Rewards Before/Now All at Once It's You/It's You Potentially Evermore."

Another team of sociologists, Irving James and Leon Mann, recently published a book called *Decision Making,* which has as its avowed purpose helping people to understand how and why decisions are made. They put the central concern of the book this way: "Psychological stress generated by a decisional conflict imposes limitations on the rationality of a person's decisions." In other words, it's hard to make good decisions under stress.

Writer-editor Malcolm Cowley, a man of exemplary courage, plunged alone and unarmed into the dense forest of prose in the *American Sociological Review*. Happily, he emerged with his mind and sentence stucture intact. He brought back reports, however, of fearsome struggles with all kinds of barbarous jargon. Early on in his journey, he encountered the phrase "ego-integrative action orientation," which momentarily reduced his mind to gruel, but he recovered and staggered on to discover that in the land of sociologese, no two things are ever said to be alike; they are "homologous" or "isomorphic." By the same token, things are never different; they are "allotropic." They are not "divided"; they are "dichotomized" or "bifurcated." Ordinary mortals like you and me occasionally speak about the "pleasure principle"; in sociologese this is transformed into "orientation toward improvement of the gratificational-deprivation balance of the actor," a phrase certain to destroy the pleasure principle in anyone who reads it.

I could go on and on taking potshots at the sociologists, but they are just one small subgroup among those notorious inhabitants of the empire of gobbledygook: the academicians. In schools and universities across the country, in the very places where monstrous language should most be avoided, word abuse reigns supreme. Even so supposedly humane a discipline as philosophy resounds with strange and inhuman noises. Consider this introduction to a book by Father Bernard Lonergan: "The aim of the present work may be bracketed by a series of disjunctions." Of course you know what disjunctions are, but just in case it's slipped your mind, I'll refresh your memory. According to Webster's, disjunctions are "the relations between two or more alternatives of a disjunctive proposition." (An example of a disjunctive proposition: "Either all men are free or no man is free.") From this definition you can tell that disjunctions are formidable beasts, not to be reckoned with lightly. And, Father Lonergan tells us, we are going to get not just one of these disjunctions, but a whole series of 'em to peruse and enjoy. What's more, he tells us, this series of disjunctions is not just lying around doing nothing; they are up and about the job of bracketing the aim of the book, or "present work." I'll bet you didn't know that an aim could be bracketed. Indeed, a second glance reveals that the aim is *not* in fact definitely bracketed, but only that it *may be* bracketed, depending on a set of circumstances that Father Lonergan coyly refuses to divulge. I am sure that by now you are anxious to rush out and buy this book, which is titled, infelicitously, *Insight.*

If you cannot locate it, then you can pick up any one of a number of other books filled with the kind of pompous, inflated, vague language that infests the groves of academe. James Degnan, of the University of Santa Clara, has called this kind of writing "the higher illiteracy," and people who speak and write this way, he says, are "straight-A illiterates." Straight-A illiterates would never dream of using a double negative or the word "irregardless." But they are illiterates nonetheless—people who have lost the ability to come out and state plainly and simply what they want to say.

Take, for example, a book on diets, promisingly entitled *Fat and Thin: A Natural History of Obesity,* by Anne Scott Beller. The title is the most comprehensible part of a book ostensibly addressed to millions of overweight Americans. Once past the title, the sentences in the book rival Marcel Proust's in length and complexity, and the author embellishes them with such terms as "frugivore," "anthropometricians," "ponderal," and "biogram." Readers, presumably, get some much-needed exercise by running to and from the dictionary. The use of such unfamiliar words is likely to persuade most of us that obesity is a recondite and mysterious business, a fat worse than death.

Then there's this passage from, of all things, a book about how to write well:

> I then invite the students to make some connections between the act of learning and the use of language: first, by asking them to consider some of the implications of an act of learning seen as an action with language—a process in which the quality of one would seem to depend on the quality of the other—and second, by asking them to examine the relation of approach to result in the context of some specific examples of the learning process.

Once a person is initiated into the society of straight-A illiterates, he finds that he can no longer stop the flow of gobbledygook that spills off his tongue, but that it will inundate every aspect of his everyday life. Last week, for example, I went to a faculty meeting at Onondaga Community College. Attendance was high because we all knew that there would be a heated discussion on one particular issue—the firing of one of the members of the music department. Before the meeting started, Mr. X., as I shall call him, circulated the following statement of his position to the rest of us:

> ### Charges
> *1. The severity of the ground upon which they reversed their own decision to reappoint me within a period of three weeks.*
>
> *2. Using extraordinary means to accomplish proceedings when such proceedings had been determined to be of such complexity that more than two months time was determined to be necessary to accomplish such ends.*

It is hard to determine from this exactly what he was fired *for*, though his statement certainly speaks for itself as to *why* he should be fired.

Semanticist Neil Postman cites the following example of straight-A illiteracy from a letter written by a schoolteacher (master's degree) to ninth-grade students:

> . . . Writers remind us constantly that with the arrival of a new year, we must become cognizant of the fact that it is time to proclaim our New Year's resolutions. As a class, let us accept for the theme of the New Year the ever-powerful meaning of the need and desire for Enthusiasm. . . . To aid and guide you on your pathway to learning, the following assignments will help you to activate vehemently your newly acquired aim, "Enthusiasm."
>
> 1. A vocabulary test will be given the day that you return to school.
>
> 2. Oral book reports will be given the first week of school.
>
> . . . I did not prepare this epistle to harass you, but . . . we must remember that reality of fact that we are beginning a program of study that will mold our future. This presents to us responsibilities . . .[4]

It is hard to believe that any student reading (the schoolteacher would probably prefer "perusing") this epistle would actually be moved to "activate vehemently" his enthusiasm—or anything else.

One of the great dangers of professorial gobbledygook is that it is so readily passed on to students and through them to the general population. Students, drowning in the academese of textbooks, soon learn survival techniques. They master the kind of "teacherspeak" that their professors want to hear, and dutifully spout back to them. Here, for example, are actual excerpts from the papers my students handed in at the beginning of the year. They had been asked to describe an interesting or unusual dream they'd had:

> The dream dealt with myself in the capacity of First Officer aboard an aircraft that had unexpectedly flown into adverse weather. The images emerged as flashbacks concerning passenger safety, crew responsibilities, and the performance of the aircraft. The dream concluded, apparently, with my awakening, and at this point I arrived at the realization that the aforementioned aircraft had effected a safe landing. . . .

> Working in a motel in the Syracuse area had afforded me the opportunity to encounter many people of varying ethnic backgrounds. Canadians, though not as ingrained in cultural traditions as, say, Italians and Spaniards, seem to represent a definite offspring of civilization, historically young though their country may be. The recent exposure to two distinct types of Canadians, these being the rural-dwelling Canadians and urban-dwelling ones, was perhaps the reason for a recent dream I experienced.

This is not the way these students normally express themselves; one can hardly imagine a young man at a bar saying to his friend, "Y'know, recent exposure to two distinct types of Canadians, these being the rural-dwelling Canadians and the urban-dwelling ones, was perhaps the reason for a recent dream I experienced." No, these are attempts to imitate the inflated, pompous prose students read in their textbooks—no matter that this prose cloaks even the simplest ideas in unnecessarily complex phraseology, no matter that it confuses rather than clarifies, no matter that it is boring to extinction: they have decided this is a desirable way to write because this is the way *educated* people write. More practically, it's a good way to impress your professor and to get an A in the course. There are other advantages: If you really perfect your skill in academese, you can get by without having really to say anything at all. Here, for example, is one student's answer to a test question on Hemingway's *Farewell to Arms*. He was asked to explain why he felt Frederick Henry, the protagonist, had decided to desert from the army. The student had not, unfortunately, read the book. That didn't stop him from answering the question:

> Every man possesses reasons for performing rash actions. Frederick Henry possesses his. Through these reasons Hemingway reveals, with searing insight and compassion, what it takes for a man to desert. I believe that this justifies Frederick Henry's desertion and leads the reader to empathize with his plight.

One cannot too much admire the ingenuity of such a student. He divined the secret of getting by in the world of academe— writing not to communicate, but just to sound important, writing not to *express* but to *impress*. A more honest student once replied to James Degnan's advice to write more simply and clearly: "If I followed your advice, I could never write the 5,000-word term papers I am regularly assigned; I could never get a fellowship to graduate school, or a contract to do a textbook, or a decent job in business or government. . . . No, I'm sorry, literacy might be okay, but I can't afford it." Incidentally, that reply is written in straightforward, admirable English, and we may mourn this young man's conversion to the illiteracy of academese.

Gobbledygook is a skill like bicycling, which, once learned, is never forgotten. To drive home that point, here is the president of our local bicycling club, a college graduate, writing in his monthly newsletter to members:

> There are three basic elements that make up what I call the bicycle unit or the complete bicyclist. These are the rider, the bicycle, and third, the facilities. Take any one of these away, and the other two elements cannot function. As for the first, with proper knowl-

edge and training, the cyclist can improve his skill as a rider. As for the second, he can demand and obtain quality equipment which is the result of many years of experience and experiment. But without the third element, the facilities, this self-sustaining unit is inoperative. Therefore, unless safe and logically planned facilities are provided, the bicycle boom in the United States will quickly come to a point of equilibrium; that is, the advancement or optimum point of the bicycle boom will be controlled by our ability to provide the facility element.[5]

The poor fellow seems to be trying to say that we need to have more bicycle paths in this country so more people can ride their bikes. Alas, he is not capable of delivering such a clear and simple message. Perhaps he was once, but that was before he went to college. The same problem obviously afflicts the president of a faculty wives club, who recently sent me a letter which began:

Dear Member:

Thanks to the outstanding weather, we have had a most enjoyable summer. Imagination and projection have been in the winds this summer for the Syracuse Women's Club and as summer ebbs, your board is looking forward with enthusiasm to the many events and ventures planned for the fall.

I'll bet you didn't know that imagination and projection could be found "in the winds," particularly since in the next sentence the winds appear to be "ebbing." This woman suffers from another symptom of "professor's disease"—overwriting in an attempt to be "poetic." Nineteenth-century Southern authors suffered chronically from this disease, which was characterized by hyperventilated "eloquence" as Mark Twain once described it:

[The Southern author] would be eloquent, or perish. And he recognized only one kind of eloquence—the lurid, the tempestuous, the volcanic. He liked words— big words, fine words, grand words, rumbling, thundering, reverberating words; with sense attaching if it could be got in without marring the sound, but not otherwise. He loved to stand up before a dazed world, and pour forth flame and smoke and lava and pumice-stone into the skies, and work his subterranean thunders, and shake himself with earthquakes, and stench himself with sulphur fumes. If he consumed his own fields and vineyards, that was a pity, yes; but he would have his eruption at any cost. . . .[6]

This disease of language is not just a nineteenth-century plague, like smallpox. The number of people afflicted by it is growing, and its progress is marked by increasing use of metaphors—particularly mixed ones. Critics and reviewers are particularly susceptible to this kind of "fancy talk." Recently, in *More* magazine, critic John Simon took fellow critic Rex Reed to task:

In perusing some of Reed's pieces in *Vogue*, I came upon some truly remarkable formulations. For example, "the note of reigning terror is struck in the first scene (a dull woman's body is being examined by a Fascist doctor) . . ." A dull corpse? How many witty ones has Reed known? But a corpse so dull as to strike a note of terror? That *is* dull, even for a corpse.

Simon quotes Reed as writing, in another review, that "the actors attacked the feast of poetry with hammers instead of chopsticks," so Simon concludes that "Poetry, clearly, is an Oriental dish." Finally, he quotes a long passage from Reed's review of *Voyage of the Damned*, a film that Reed loved:

[The passengers of the ship] "are joined in a common

bond of hope. Their joyless fates hang in the balance while the heartless structures of diplomatic red tape barter for them like cattle at a livestock show, yet they dance to Glenn Miller's 'Moonlight Serenade.'"

Of this, Simon remarks:

"A common bond of hope" sounds rather inspiriting; but no, these are joyless fates that hang in the balance. If, however, they are already defined as joyless, what kind of balance can they still hang in? Perhaps that common bond of hope is actually wound around their necks. Meanwhile, heartless structures are bartering for them. Has a structure ever had a heart, to say nothing of it bartering? But this is a structure of red tape; something like a card castle, I assume, only made of tape instead of cards. These tape structures are bartering like cattle at a livestock show, while the traders, I suppose, stand by tethered and mooing.[7]

The New York Times once described Reed's prose as a series of "deliciously muddled metaphors" and concluded that verbal gaucheries are his trademark, for "Mr. Reed is the Rhinestone Cowboy of journalism." Like the president of the bicycle club and the woman who writes for the Syracuse Women's Club, Reed obviously believes that in writing for publication, fancy phrases and impressive-sounding language count for more than what he is actually talking about. The result is the kind of writing that is always crossing the Rubicon and discovering that it has no place to go. Fewer and fewer people realize that what really counts in writing is exactly the same thing that counts in talking—the ability to express yourself as clearly, directly, and gracefully as possible.

Every year our language becomes more and more encrusted with the pale cast of gobbledygook. One day plain English may vanish from the world, leaving behind only a lot of specialized vocabularies. Then the biblical Tower of Babel will become an accurate description of a world in which the great mass of humanity can no longer communicate with each other. Gobbledygook will triumph, and even the simplest nursery rhyme will be transformed. Here is an excerpt from *Poor Russell's Almanac*, in which Russell Baker shows how a simple rhymed tale might be rendered incomprehensible in a variety of different styles of gobbledygook:

Little Miss Muffet, as everyone knows, sat on a tuffet eating her curds and whey, when along came a spider, and sat down beside her, and frightened Miss Muffet away. While everyone knows this, the significance of the event had never been analyzed until a conference of thinkers recently brought their special insights to bear upon it. Following are excerpts from the transcript of their discussions:

Book Reviewer: Written on several levels, this searing and sensitive exploration of the arachnid heart illuminates the agony and splendor of Jewish family life with a candor that is at once breathtaking in its simplicity and soul-shattering in its implied ambiguity. Some will doubtless be shocked to see such subjects as tuffets and whey discussed without flinching, but hereafter writers too timid to call a curd a curd will no longer . . .

Sociologist: We are clearly dealing here with a prototypical illustration of a highly tensile social structure's tendency to dis- or perhaps even de-structure itself under the pressures created when optimum minimums do not obtain among the disadvantaged. Miss Muffet is nutritionally underprivileged, as evidenced by the subminimal diet of curds and whey upon which she is forced to subsist, while the spider's cultural disadvantage is evidenced by such phenomena as legs exceeding standard norms, odd mating habits, and so forth.

In this instance, spider expectations lead the culturally disadvantaged to assert demands to share the tuffet with the nutritionally underprivileged. Due to a communications failure, Miss Muffet assumes without evidence that the spider will not be satisfied to share her tuffet, but will also insist on eating her curds and perhaps even her whey. Thus the failure to preestablish selectively optimum norm structures diverts potentially optimal minimums from the expectation levels assumed to . . .

Militarist: Second-strike capability, sir! That's what was lacking. If Miss Muffet had developed a second-strike capability instead of squandering her resources on curds and whey, no spider on earth would have dared launch a first strike capable of carrying him right to the heart of her tuffet. I am confident that Miss Muffet had adequate notice from experts that she could not afford both curds and whey and, at the same time, support an early-warning system. Yet curds alone were not good enough for Miss Muffet. She had to have whey, too. Tuffet security must be the first responsibility of every diner. . . .

Psychiatrist: Little Miss Muffet is, of course, neither little nor a miss. These are obviously the self she has created in her own fantasies to escape the reality that she is a gross divorcée whose superego makes it impossible for her to sustain a normal relationship with any man, symbolized by the spider, who, of course, has no existence outside her fantasies. Little Miss Muffet may, in fact, be a man with deeply repressed Oedipal impulses, who sees in the spider the father he would like to kill, and very well may some day unless he admits that what he believes to be a tuffet is, in fact, probably the dining room chandelier, and that the whey he thinks he is eating is, in fact, probably . . .

Child: This is about a little girl who gets scared by a spider.

(The child was sent home when the conference broke for lunch. It was agreed that he was too immature to subtract anything from the sum of human understanding.)[8]

3

Get Your Facts First—
Then Distort 'Em All You Like

*The manner of your speaking is full as important as the
matter, as more people have ears to be tickled than un-
derstandings to judge.*

Chesterfield

The other day, I picked up a copy of our local Syracuse newspaper and saw this headline: "WILL STATE TAXPAYERS BE
FORCED TO BAIL OUT NEW YORK CITY?" As a state taxpayer,
it was hard to remain unmoved by the question. Its implica-
tions were clear enough: I would be "forced" by sinister
agencies beyond my control to "bail out" a criminal city that
richly deserved the trouble it was in. Why should I and all the
other decent, frugal, overburdened taxpayers of New York
State be required to sacrifice our hard-earned tax dollars for
the sake of a recreant, spendthrift, "bad boy" city? The pros-
pect must have caused Syracuse readers to swear over their
coffee cups that morning.

Let's consider alternative ways the same idea might have
been expressed. What if the headline had read, "WILL STATE
TAXPAYERS BE ASKED TO HELP OUT NEW YORK CITY IN TIME
OF CRISIS?" The whole proposition sounds more palatable
that way. Or what if the headline had included the phrase
"COMING TO THE AID OF NEW YORK CITY"? How about
"LENDING A NEIGHBORLY HAND" or "BEING A GOOD SAMARI-

TAN," which would stack the deck in *favor* of aid to New York?

Newspaper headlines, because of their brevity, depend heavily on the writer's interpretation of the event. As A. J. Liebling, the late contributor to *The New Yorker,* said, "Different reporters see different things, or the same things differently." When we were at war in Vietnam, a reader's idea of how things were going depended on what paper he was reading. On one day, *The New York Times* read, "IN HANOI, LEADERS AND PUBLIC SEEM CONFIDENT." The same day, the cover headline of *U.S. News & World Report* read, "NORTH VIETNAM: PLIGHT OF THE ENEMY . . . HAIPHONG IS RUINED AND RAVAGED." Probably the only way to get a clear idea of the situation would have been to read both reports and draw your own conclusions. Bill Moyers, Press Secretary to Lyndon Johnson, gives an example of the time Edwin O. Reischauer resigned as United States Ambassador to Japan. Reischauer was interviewed by the press, and the following day the headline in the *Washington Post* read, "REISCHAUER BACKS U.S. VIET POLICY." The headline in *The New York Times* read, REISCHAUER CRITICAL OF VIETNAM POLICY." Someone had to be talking to the wrong Edwin O. Reischauer.

The contradiction in these headlines is not much of a problem to someone who has more than one news source: the differences can probably be reconciled by a careful reading of two or more versions. But in eighty-five percent of American cities, the citizens have only one newspaper, which means that most of us get only one account of a news story. This, according to A. J. Liebling, is like "having a Gallup Poll with only one straw."

The Associated Press prides itself on being a perfectly "objective" and "reliable" news source. AP supplies the news stories to newspapers and broadcasting studios across the nation, who rely on the news service to give them a straight, unbiased, "bare-bones" account. "Our stories are the closest

thing there is to the plain, unvarnished truth of the matter,"
says an AP spokesman. Yet this very emphasis on "objectivity" sometimes results in an unwitting bias. Writer Fred Pow-
ledge tells the story of one occasion when this happened. During the U.S. invasion of Cambodia (always referred to by the
AP as an "incursion"), Peter Arnett, a Pulitzer prizewinning
journalist, was covering the story for AP. Arnett was with the
U.S. troops when they entered one town and looted it, and he
dutifully reported the entire incident. When the story arrived
at AP headquarters in New York City, the description of the
looting was taken out. When Arnett heard about the cut, he
was furious and demanded an explanation. AP headquarters
sent this cable in reply:

> WE ARE IN THE MIDST OF A HIGHLY CHARGED SITUA-
> TION IN UNISTATES REGARDING SOUTHEAST ASIA AND
> MUST GUARD OUR COPY TO SEE THAT IT IS DOWN THE
> MIDDLE AND SUBDUES EMOTION. SPECIFICALLY TO-
> DAY WE TOOK LOOTING AND SIMILAR REFERENCES
> OUT OF ARNETT COPY BECAUSE WE DON'T THINK IT'S
> ESPECIALLY NEWS THAT SUCH THINGS TAKE PLACE IN
> WAR AND IN PRESENT CONTEXT THIS CAN BE INFLAM-
> MATORY.

Clearly, AP felt that the best way to be "objective" was to
steer opinion "down the middle." But the very act of steering
opinion, no matter in which direction, defeats the ideal of objectivity. The cable makes it quite clear that AP feels its job is
to *decide* what is news and what is not—and that, of course,
items adjudged to be "not news" will be omitted. Here reality
is being shaped not so much by the choice of words as by the
selection of detail. People who read about soldiers looting get
a different view of the war from people who don't. Is it really
"objective" to make judgments like these about what is appropriate for us to know and what isn't? No, says Professor
of Journalism David Feldman, who has made a long study of

slanting and bias in the news: "News is not news if it is condensed, reworked, edited and carefully selected. It is something else, but it is not a true reflection of the event."

Newsmagazines are probably the worst offenders. Magazines like *Time, Newsweek,* and *U.S. News & World Report* pose as objective analysts of the news but in fact engage heavily in what might be called "interpretive reporting." That is, they not only report the news, they make judgments on it; they tell the reader not only what is happening, but how to feel about it. For example, here is the lead article from *Newsweek* magazine for the week of February 21, 1977:

> For Jimmy Carter, it was another week given heavily over to the politics of imagery—a show-and-tell attempt to make the Presidency his own and make America like it. He spent his days in restless public motion . . . dashing to pep rallies at four Cabinet departments, strewing his trail with further thoughts of Chairman Jimmy on matters ranging from service in government to sex out of wedlock.

The language of the article carefully creates the impression that Carter's activities during the week were all part of a show-biz attempt to win over the American public—and not the serious work of statecraft. Carter, we are told, had "pep rallies" with four Cabinet departments. Why not "meetings" or "conferences"? "Pep rallies" sounds like high-school stuff—the coach meeting with the football squad to get everyone charged up for the game. "Restless" motion has the suggestion that all this activity was nervously unproductive—again, the "all-show-and-no-substance" idea. Carter, we are told, has been "strewing his trail" (sounds messy and incautious) with "thoughts of Chairman Jimmy." The comparison to Chairman Mao Tse-tung is obvious; the implication is that Jimmy Carter expects from the American people the same kind of reverence for his pronouncements as the Chinese showed for Mao's. "What arrogance," the reader is likely to conclude. "Who the hell is he to inflict his thoughts about sex out of wedlock on me!" This is the kind of slanted, card-stacking, interpretive reportage that passes for "news," or objective fact, because it appears in a "news" magazine. In fact, a different observer could have reported on Carter's activities that week quite differently. During the week of February 21, Carter held an extensive news conference in which he fielded some important questions about foreign affairs, campaigned actively and successfully in the Congress to head off strong opposition to his government-reorganization bill, and proposed a change in the existing tax structure that would dramatically cut taxes for families earning less than $16,000 a year, while raising them for families earning more. Here's how the same article might look if it had focused on these events, and omitted the negatively charged language:

> For Jimmy Carter, it was a week given heavily over to matters of state. He spent his days in tireless motion—presiding over conferences at four Cabinet departments, holding an extensive news conference in which he outlined his position on matters ranging from government service to simple morality, and campaigning vigorously for support of his bold government-reorganization bill.

This version, of course, tips the scales in Carter's favor. Both this and *Newsweek*'s version give the reader no chance to make up his own mind about the "news": he is presented with a chewed-over, predigested interpretation of the week's events. No wonder Bill Moyers has said, "Of all the great myths of American journalism, objectivity is the greatest. What is happening depends on who is looking."

This kind of word abuse in newsmagazines is often communicated in very subtle ways. For example, a character's name can be prefaced with one or two adjectives describing him unfavorably, such as "jowly, sunken-eyed Barry," "thin, nervous-looking Ramsey," or "large, loud-voiced Bella." Verbs are negatively slanted, too—particularly synonyms of "to talk" or "to say." "Thin, nervous-looking Ramsey squeaked out a protest," or "Large, loud-voiced Bella shrieked her defiance," paints a damning picture without the appearance of direct criticism. When *Time* magazine was still under the editorship of its founder, Henry B. Luce, it often used this technique to slant opinion. People Luce disapproved of rarely "said" or "stated" anything; they tended to "cry" or "cry out." Other people whom Luce disliked were characterized as "snorting," "snarling," "sputtering," and "spouting." Prime Minister Nehru, whom Luce detested, was described as "croaking throatily." In reverse, people of whom Luce approved always "stated solemnly," or "quipped," "laughed," and "joked." It was the same when people walked. The bad guys "popped out," "flounced," "crept," and sometimes even "weaseled." The good guys—in particular Luce's hero, President Eisenhower—always "strode."

These insidious practices are alive and well on the pages of current newsmagazines. Alexander Cockburn, a journalist and sometime foreign correspondent, has laid down tongue-in-cheek guidelines for the "proper adjectival adornment for leaders":

> . . . . if he is one of *our* dictators, then use words like "dynamic," "strong man," "able." He "laughs" a great deal, is always "on the move," "in a hurry." He "brushes impatiently aside" questions about franchise and civil liberties: "My people are not yet ready for these amenities you in the West feel free to enjoy. . . ."
>
> If, on the other hand, he is one of *their* dictators, then use words like "unstable," "brooding," "erratic," "bloodthirsty," "indolent." He seldom ventures out of his palace unless under "heavy guard." He is "rumored to be ailing. . . ." [1]

Another insidious form of word abuse practiced by news-magazines is the subjective narrative style, a kind of dramatic scene-setting that "fictionalizes" news stories to give them human interest. For example, when Thomas P. ("Tip") O'Neill became Speaker of the House of Representatives, *Newsweek* ran this cover story:

> He is a bricklayer's son, a husky man with silver hair who stood before the House of Representatives last week in his best gray-flannel suit. His wife, Mildred, beamed down at him from the members' gallery. Out in Statuary Hall, 500 old pals, pols, guests, and maybe a bookie or two from Boston cheered as his image flashed on closed-circuit TV. As he mounted the speaker's platform, he paused and swallowed hard. . . .

Tip O'Neill sounds more like a character in a novel than a real person. The article is titled, "The Man of the House," in the suggestive way of a fiction story. All that is really being said, of course, is that Tip O'Neill got up and gave a speech accepting his election as Speaker of the House. But the writer manages to communicate much more than that. There is an artfully created image of O'Neill as an average, unassuming man, nervous and yet a bit moved by the honor that has been bestowed on him. Is this the real Tip O'Neill? How much is the image created by the wordsmith?

Anyone can be given this kind of artful, humanizing write-up:

> He is a pensioner's son, a man of less than medium height, with slightly unruly hair. He walked up to the platform that day with the brisk, purposeful step of a man with a mission, and stood blinking against the glare of the bright midday sun. The crowd roared its love for this solitary, dedicated man. For a long moment, he did not, could not speak; it was obvious that

his own emotions were deeply touched. He had come a long way to reach this plateau.

That happens to be a word picture of Adolf Hitler.

Newswriters too often use the poetic license of fiction while wrapping themselves in the mantle of objectivity. This may make their copy livelier and more appealing, but the ideal of news reporting becomes a mere masquerade. The basic question is: Should the news entertain or should it inform? If facts are so overlaid with colorful interpretation, how can we recognize the facts? As Walker Gibson, an acute observer of this phenomenon, says, "If the alternative to dullness is dishonesty, it may be better to be dull."

Dullness is simply not a conceivable alternative to editors responsible for keeping the circulation of their magazines in the multimillions. To them, dullness, not dishonesty, is the unforgivable sin. As one newsmagazine editor commented after reading the foregoing passage, "If we gave the public straight hard news, they wouldn't become more knowledgeable. They'd simply stop reading."

Indeed, millions of people *have* stopped reading even the "slanted" news in leading newspapers and newsmagazines simply because it is "hard news"—which can be reinterpreted as "hard to read." No matter how intriguingly this kind of news is written, these readers aren't interested in the basic subject matter. They want gossip, personalized news stories, shock, highly embroidered and fanciful accounts of incidents that may never actually have happened.

And where do they get their news?

Tabloids

Viscount Northcliff, the noted English newspaperman, once advised journalists to "Never lose your sense of the superficial," and tabloid sheets (they can hardly be classified as newspapers) have been dutifully following his advice ever since. Tabloids make no pretense of reporting real news; it's far too uninteresting. They look for whatever in the news can be written up into a narrative of action and excitement, preferably a disaster, at least a scandal. The problem, of course, is that there just aren't enough disasters or scandals in the world to keep the pages of the tabloids filled. So the tabloid writer has to create them. This is why tabloid writers are skilled in the art of exaggerating without actually lying. In the language of the tabloids, every action is "drastic," every decision "crucial," every defeat "crushing." Take, for example, this story quoted by Alexander Cockburn from the front page of a tabloid:

RACE THROUGH HELL FIRE:
Train Passengers Run Oil Blaze Gauntlet

A crowded train raced past a wall of flame last night as fire swept through an oil tanker train only feet away. . . . The express . . . went by minutes after the tanker train exploded into flames . . . Mrs. Clare Hicks, a passenger on the express, said, ". . . The flames were very close. We could feel the heat inside the train." . . . Houses in Meadowfield Road and Mead Road came within feet of total destruction. For just 30 feet from the blazing train were six giant storage tanks filled with fuel. Said a senior fire officer, "If that lot had gone up, the explosion would have destroyed the whole village . . . "[2]

As you can see, nothing actually happened—that is, no one was killed, no one was injured, the train was not even delayed. But the tabloid writer has worked the story up nicely, with all sorts of ominous intimations of what *might* have happened had things been just a little different. A splendid example of how to snatch disaster from the jaws of safety.

Of course, if a tabloid writer is lucky enough to stumble on a *real* disaster, then he can really go to town. Cockburn laid down the following "guidelines" for maximally effective disaster reporting:

> FLOODS: Pictures crucial. Always have people perched on rooftops, cows with noses above water. Also pictures and stories on people who have lost all . . . Floods are *always* rising and therefore stress frantic urgency of hold-off operations. Families sandbagging their homes, engineers manfully building dikes. . . . Good chance for stylists to brood on "swollen, sullen flood" which is usually "silt-brown" and invariably has some dead cows and horses in it.
>
> AVALANCHES: Emphasize "frantic rescuers clawing at the snow." Also get accounts of survivors and remember to have one of them say, "There was a crack like a pistol shot and then a terrifying roar. Then it was on us." Stress risk of further avalanches in the area which can be set off by the slightest sound . . . . Imply negligence of local authorities in not heeding warnings of sage mountain folk. Stick around till the bodies are dug out. It is a virtual certainty that one of the doomed skiers took a photograph of the avalanche seconds before it engulfed him. Thus: Last Snaps of a Doomed Man . . . .
>
> TORNADOES: Stress malign fury and awesome strength of the twister, "hurling cars hundreds of yards, tearing up houses . . . " Emphasize miraculous escape of child in pram. Ask where it will strike next. . . .
>
> HURRICANES: Remember that a hurricane is always nearing a major population center. Get a pilot to fly through if possible. With any luck you will have a terrific devastation story to follow through with. Remember to have "winds of up to 150 miles per hour." Remember that this may be the chance for a record. Is it the worst hurricane in living memory?[3]

Unfortunately, the tabloid writer can't count on getting lucky like this. There are bound to be days when there's just not a disaster or even a near disaster to be scraped up. That's when the writer must start thinking about a suitable scandal to fill the front page. Tabloid reports on scandals, like reports on disaster, have deliberate exaggeration and sensationalism as the keynote. In the language of the tabloid, if a woman is under fifty, she is "young"; if she is ordinary-looking, she is "attractive"; and if she is really ugly, she is referred to simply as a "blonde" or a "redhead." If she has no discernible occupation, she becomes a "model" or a "socialite." This helps perk up reader interest in her problems. Using these simple guidelines, we can come up with a fine tabloid headline like : "SPANIARD SLAYS GLAMOROUS REDHEAD IN LOVE NEST," which in reality means, "DRUNK KILLS 50-YR-OLD FORMER CLEANING LADY IN ROUTE 12 MOTEL."

"CARTER'S KILLER NANNY TALKS!!" screamed a recent tabloid headline. What a splendid piece of copy. See how cleverly it plays to the reader's lurid interests—the idea of a "killer" nanny in the White House is agreeably suggestive of a woman who poses as a household servant only to turn around and slaughter her little charges at the first opportune moment. To say that this "killer" nanny "talks" adds the perfect touch, suggesting some kind of criminal confession. Perhaps the killer nanny will describe a past slaughter of the innocents in suitably livid detail? The only way to find out, of course, is to buy the paper, because killer nanny does not get around to "talking" on the front page. The last words on the front page are "I don't try to justify what I did. What I did was . . ." (story cont. on page 5). On page 5, we learn that what she did was ". . . wrong. I'm just so happy these fine people had the faith to give me a second chance." The killer nanny continues to "talk" for two more columns—about how nice the Carter family is to work for, and how interesting it is to see the inside of the White House. *That's all.* Nary a bloody knife nor a mutilated body to be found. The stories inside the tabloids never do add up to very much. But that doesn't matter, as long as the headlines can sucker enough people into buying the paper. (Worst example of a sucker headline ever recorded was in a fan magazine: "WHY TONY CURTIS WILL NEVER MARRY." The answer, you found after you paid the quarter, is that there is no Tony Curtis, since his real name is Bernard Schwartz!)

Television News

For all their shortcomings, newspapers do, at least, have great advantages over television, as Marya Mannes points out:

> They can be used by men as barriers against their wives. The newspaper is still the only effective screen against the morning features of the loved one, and, as such, performs a unique human service. The second advantage is that you can't line a garbage pail with a television set—it's usually the other way around.[4]

And as James Reston puts it, "One of the great things about a newspaper is that . . . you can throw away what you don't want, and the ads don't sing."

A more serious advantage is that reading the written word stimulates sequential, logical thought, and gives the reader a chance to *think* about what he is learning. The short narratives (sometimes as little as one paragraph) that accompany pictorial items in a typical TV news broadcast invite a sensory, emotional response. People who rely exclusively on TV news for their information rarely have any understanding of the background of current events. How many Americans ever really understood the nature and cause of the conflict in Northern Ireland or the war in Angola? One reason may be the *way* the news was presented to them on TV. The TV news audience rarely gets any sustained explanation or argument from its newscasters—just isolated, disconnected bits of detail. Take the war in Angola, for example. American TV viewers got brief flashes of marching troops, of an antiaircraft battery in action, of a grieving mother being led weeping from the gravesite of her dead son, of a city street blocked off and barricades manned by armed partisans. But few of us ever learned *why* these battles were raging, these mothers grieving, these city streets turned into armed camps. When I took a random poll of several persons-on-the-street to see if they knew what the fighting in Angola was about, their answers were revealing: "Aren't they fighting over religion?" "We're trying to stop the Russians over there." "It has something to do with Fidel Castro." I suppose that an eighteenth-century Chinese who had gotten his information from a TV news broadcast might equally well have said that the cause of our Revolutionary War was the exorbitant price of tea.

Part of the reason for the lack of in-depth analysis in the day's television news is the inordinate pressure of on-the-scene reporting. A TV reporter on the scene in southern Lebanon, with Israeli and Palestinian machine guns rat-tat-tatting all around him, has no time, and even less inclination, to regale his listeners with an enlightening history of the struggle to date. Often, he doesn't have time to check out the facts he's reporting right that minute, which may be based on nothing more than rumors and reports from unreliable sources. The TV viewer is the victim of this kind of reporting, which offers hasty generalizations and oversimplifications instead of the full story. Literary critic Gilbert Highet sums up the dangers of news editing when he says that "To simplify history is to falsify it."

TV newsmen are sensitive to any criticism of on-the-scene reporting. "Given the difficulties of reporting under stress like this," says Walter Cronkite, "it's remarkable that on-the-scene reporters do as well, by and large, as they do." That's probably true. On-the-scene reporters do yeoman's work in a tough job. But that's beside the point. They are still, willy-nilly, practitioners of word abuse.

What can the TV-news watcher rely on if he is not getting *all* the facts? He can rely on the anchorperson, of course. Walter Cronkite or John Chancellor or David Brinkley or

Frank Reynolds will pull it all together into a coherent, seamless piece toward which the viewer can have an attitude of some kind. But this raises another question: How far can we trust the anchor people to give us the news untainted by personal opinion—even if expressed only in the tone of voice or the lift of an eyebrow?

Walter Cronkite once remarked that "the distinguishing mark of the professional journalist is that he can set aside his personal opinions in reporting the day's news." That's wishful distinguishing. It's asking too much to expect a person to set aside a "personal" opinion. Even if his heart is as pure as driven snow, and his desire to be objective is equal to that of ten ordinary mortals, he's bound to reveal his bias through the words he chooses to shape his thought. Consciously or unconsciously, a reporter interprets the news he reports.

Newscaster David Brinkley comes right out and admits it: "Objectivity is impossible to a normal human being. To be 'objective' is to be a vegetable." His explanation of what constitutes news is equally honest: "News is what *I* say it is. It's something worth knowing by *my* standards." Discomfiting, certainly, but true. News *is* what the people who write the news decide it should be. The TV viewing audience accepts their sketchy summaries as representative of the Whole Truth, or The Facts of the Matter. Yet some of the most important information is what is left *un*said.

Much *has* to remain unsaid due to the pressures of limited time. Right now, the average news program runs just under twenty-two minutes, allowing for commercials and other interruptions. The total number of words spoken in a typical news broadcast fills only a little less than half a newspaper page—about three columns, to be exact. A recent study of network news called it a "headline service with some pictorial coverage." In order to fit complicated stories into the available time, TV newswriters have to simplify and omit so much that meaning is often obliterated. For example, a recent broadcast on the NBC network station in New York City

showed graphic photographs of abandoned tenement buildings, attributing the devastation to the effects of rent control.
Landlords who couldn't make a profit on these buildings were
leaving them to their miserable fate, the newscaster informed
us. What he did *not* mention was that similar areas of abandoned buildings exist in every large city in America or that, in
fact, New York City ranks tenth on the list of cities afflicted
with this problem. And the nine other cities ahead of New
York on the list do not have any form of rent control at all!

This is the kind of reportage that even the most devout de-
fender of television news would admit is distortion through
omission. TV newsmen fight a battle with the clock every
night. The most complex and multifaceted legislative propos-
als have to be distilled into a brief seventy-five- or ninety-
second report. Ron Nessen, former President Ford's press
secretary and previously a TV newsman himself, complained
about this recently:

> At 10 a.m. a network correspondent at the White
> House may be handed, say, a legislative proposal con-
> sisting of several hundred pages of legal jargon, expla-
> nation, charts and background.
>
> By 6:30 that evening, the correspondent must try to re-
> duce that to a script of 200 words or so, explaining
> what the proposal would do, why it was made and
> what's the outlook for approval by Congress.[5]

CBS newsman Dan Rather calls this "an impossible task,"
which may explain why more and more stories that require
careful analysis and explanation are simply being omitted entirely from network news.

Omission is, in fact, the most effective and insidious form
of word abuse practiced by television news. That's because
people have no way of knowing what things have been omitted from that night's broadcast. On TV, there are no blank

spaces to indicate that something is missing. And the stories that do remain are overemphasized in importance relative to the rest of what happened that day. Increasingly, too, the stories that are chosen reflect the television industry's desperate struggle for ratings. Dan Rather has observed that television's need for pictures to accompany a story usually plays a role in the kind of news story chosen for telecast.

There is also a certain whimsicality in the way networks choose the stories they report. During the week of March 7–11, 1977, there were fifteen stories that ABC and CBS carried that NBC did not. And NBC carried five stories that were not covered by the other two networks. Local news stations are worse. Professor Jack Lyle made a study of the news as reported one week by seven different television stations in Los Angeles. He found that the seven stations carried a total of 103 stories, only 5 of which appeared on all seven, and 65 of which appeared on only one station. As Robert Cirino, author of *Don't Blame the People*, observed, there is a definite "capriciousness in the selections which determine for the public their view of the world for one day."

The viewer watching NBC gets a very different view of the world from the viewer watching CBS the very same night. On March 11, 1977, James Schlesinger, President Carter's energy adviser, gave testimony before a Senate committee about the President's proposal to set up a new Department of Energy. The reporters assigned to cover the story for NBC said that Schlesinger's testimony "didn't amount to anything." But reporters assigned to CBS and ABC thought his ideas were important, and that night both networks broadcast full tape reports on his appearance, focusing on his remarks that Americans would have to adjust to real shortages and inconveniences in the very near future.

Omission isn't the only way TV news can shape reality. The order in which stories are broadcast determines how important they will appear to the viewer. A "lead" story—the one that opens the broadcast—is always seen as the most significant news of the day. Yet there are many days when each of the three major networks leads off with a different story— which means viewers get one of three different views of reality, depending on which channel they are tuned to. Eric Levin did a study of the order of news stories on the three networks on one day in March 1977 and reported:

> ABC and CBS each led with a report on [Yitzhak] Rabin's first day of talks with Carter. . . . Much lower in the order, around the middle of the CBS show, Cronkite read a short item reporting that the Port Authority of New York had postponed a decision on whether to lift the ban on use of Kennedy Airport by the British/French Concorde. The delay would give Concorde engineers time to submit new plans for lessening the intense noise the plane generates on takeoff and landing. At ABC, roughly at the same place on the show, Harry Reasoner read a similar item. Neither network thought the story merited more than that. . . .
>
> NBC led with the Concorde story. It opened with Robert Hagar at Kennedy, then switched to John Palmer in Paris for a report on the vehement public protest in England and France against the Port Authority's recalcitrance. Finally, Chancellor and David Brinkley asked Palmer some additional questions, a feature NBC calls "cross talk" . . . Rabin—the lead at ABC and CBS—was played third by NBC.[6]

So, in effect, if you were watching NBC that night, you would think that the controversy over the Concorde was of major importance, threatening an international upheaval between the United States and her closest allies. Carter's conference with Rabin would seem relatively unimportant, just another round in the endless game of diplomacy. If you were watching CBS or ABC, the Rabin story would sound like the most significant world event, a major conference in a year that could be the one in which Arabs and Israelis would at last strike a peace. The Concorde story would appear to be a minor incident concerning airport policies. No wonder John Lane, senior producer at CBS news, says, "Judging news is a very imprecise science." The decision about what is newsworthy and what isn't often boils down to a mere matter of a newscaster's personal tastes and interests.

The problem of limited time and the pressures of on-the-scene reporting are inherent in the medium of TV and there is little anyone can do about it. There is something, however, that news stations can do to give their audience a less distorted view of the world. That is to halt the growing trend toward "human interest" stories. With news time already so limited, it seems a shame to waste it on stories about Amy Carter's school day, as in this recent broadcast described by Ron Nessen:

> Barbara Walters . . . interviewed Rosalynn Carter for two minutes and 18 seconds on the subject of which school Amy would attend in Washington.
> That's a lot of time, considering Barbara and Harry have only about 22 minutes to tell *all* the news.
> But wait.
> The interview is followed by a correspondent named Jim Kincaid delivering an inane open letter to Amy about her new school:
> Dear Amy,
> You may not remember me . . . I heard that your Daddy got that Government job he was looking for . . . Your teacher, Mrs. Meeder, is neat and doesn't get mad or anything like that . . .
> Your friend, Jim Kincaid

Kincaid's report lasts just over two and one-half minutes. So now, about one-sixth of the entire evening news has been devoted to Amy's school.
But wait.
Barbara comes back with another two minutes and

32 seconds of hot tidbits from her recent trip to Plains, Georgia: Amy reads *Rebecca of Sunnybrook Farm* during church services, and Jimmy Carter, "like a good Daddy," returns to church to retrieve Amy's misplaced coat.

Thus, the 15 million Americans who tuned in to the ABC Evening News to find out what happened in the world that day were told, in effect, that one-third of all the news worthy of their attention involved Amy Carter.[7]

David Broder, correspondent for the *Washington Post*, has called this kind of reporting "trivialization" of news, and proposes a remedy, to wit, "For every feature story on Billy Carter, the newspaper or network responsible would be required to run a full-scale analysis of zero-based budgeting and the report of Mr. Carter's task force on government reorganization." Mr. Broder's proposal is unlikely to go far. The trend of many news programs today is in the opposite direction. They discard what's important in favor of what's "interesting." A recent broadcast on CBS had two long human interest stories, one on a man who had walked across the frozen lake near his home (the reporter hastened to point out that it had begun to defrost, and had the man fallen in, he would have frozen to death in a mere sixty seconds) and one on a high-school basketball team that had to *lose* a game to the visiting team in order to qualify for the play-offs. "There is a real danger of distortion whenever news is forced to meet the demands of entertainment," says Jim Mackillop, a longtime observer of the news media.

Nevertheless, Ron Powers, a Pulitzer Prizewinning television critic, believes the trend toward entertainment is steadily accelerating. In his book *The Newscasters*, Mr. Powers argues that TV journalism is increasingly governed by the values and standards of show business, toward "what gratifies as opposed to what is useful or necessary." The selection of news, he contends, is determined not by qualified journalists but by a growing swarm of "experts" who claim to have discovered what the public would like to see and hear. Mr. Powers cites an organization called Entertainment Response Analysts (ERA) that tests viewers' conscious and unconscious reactions with electrodes that measure the galvanic skin response to particular anchormen, staff reporters, weather forecasters, sportscasters. ERA promises to deliver to its television clients "the hard facts about what works and what doesn't, what communicates and what irritates, who is effective and what kind of writing, film editing, sequencing and pacing works best." The goal of such electronic analysis is to point the way to the Ultima Thule of higher audience ratings and increased advertising revenues.

In response to ERA's findings, news programs have begun to emphasize stories on crime, catastrophes, and celebrities, and to deemphasize stories on local government, pending legislation, and political interviews. More attention is paid to the decor of sets, the colors, and the hairstyles and attire of the newscasters. If news producers continue to follow the recommendations of entertainment consultants, professional journalists may soon be pushed aside entirely in favor of Handsome Harry types. Today's newscasters, seeing the handwriting on the wall, are already nervous. Dan Rather is worried that his face is too impassive, and feels that he should probably punctuate news bulletins with a smile more frequently. John Chancellor frets about his staid demeanor and his dreary monotone. Harry Reasoner feared that his underplayed witticisms might not find a large enough audience—and was proved right when Barbara Walters was brought in to share his anchor spot, and the clash of their very different styles was a ratings disaster.

But entertainment news hasn't triumphed yet. One reassuring note was the short-lived tenure of the so-called "Happy News" programs on local television programs. Instead of providing information, these programs were designed to exude warmth, charm, and good humor. "You like us because *we* like us" was the slogan of WABC-TV's news program in New York. The individual reporters, carefully attired in colorful blazers, smiled and laughed frequently, made jokes, cut silly capers, exchanged witty ad-libs, and in general did what they could to enliven with cheerful banter the often gloomy and depressing reports of what was happening in the world. This often led to some unsettling juxtapositions:

> Tom: Hurricane Martha raged through the tiny town of Fall River, Massachusetts, today, leaving in its wake millions of dollars worth of property damage. At least twelve people have been found dead, and the death toll is expected to rise as rescue operations continue. Over to you, John.
>
> John: Thanks, Tom. Gee, that's too bad about Fall River City. But at least we're having wonderful weather here, eh?
>
> Tom: Oh, you bet. (*Cheerily*) It's been just beautiful. We're planning on going out to the lake to take the kids sailing this weekend.
>
> John: Great idea. Nothing like being near the water in springtime, I always say. Well, Tom, here's a late-breaking story about the drowning death of a twenty-eight-year-old Springfield housewife . . .

Fortunately, viewers were jarred by the tasteless linking of floods and funnies, and Happy News went to its grave, presumably still smiling.

Nevertheless, the danger is not past. As long as competition for ratings continues to dominate the world of television, no one can be sure news will not be turned into a "celebrity business," as Dan Rather fears. One can envision John Chancellor being replaced by Chevy Chase, or Walter Cronkite by Rich Little—who would doubtless deliver the news in a variety of different personas. Perhaps Barbara could work up a little tap dance to lead the viewer merrily, imperceptibly, into the *Laverne and Shirley* show.

4

**They Couldn't Say It
If It Weren't True**

It's a great art to know how to sell wind.

Confucius

Whenever people get around to discussing the power of words, admen invariably are cast as the Savonarolas of the Western world—the fervid, fanatic magicians whose job it is to stir up emotions and befog the thinking of the masses, so they will rush out, willy-nilly, and buy, buy, *buy*.

Admen, of course, laugh at this idea. "It's ridiculous," one Madison Avenue advertising executive told me. "This whole idea that we can somehow force people to buy things they don't want is just stupid. If someone objects to a particular product or to the way it is advertised, all he has to do is stop buying it. That's the power of the pocketbook. It's the consumer who's got all the cards up his sleeve, not the ad agencies."

Not so. Admen are not magicians, but they cast very potent spells. For the power of a spell, as all magicians from Merlin to Blackstone have known, is the power of the word. In Tolkien's classic, *The Lord of the Rings*, Gandalf, the most fearsome magician in all of Eriador, intones magical gibberish, "Naur an edraith ammen! Naur dan i ngaurhoth!" and the

91

gathered crowd sways to his command. Today's adman does the same thing, but his spell sounds more like, "New! Improved! Limited Time Only!" Next time we are in the supermarket, we obey. We pick up a carton of Downy Fabric Softener or Easy-Off Oven Cleaner or whatever. For admen are word manipulators—as columnist Melvin Madocks says, they are "the carnival barkers of life who misuse language to pitch and con and make the quick kill."

Few of us admit to being conned. We all think it's the *other* guy who's being suckered. Jeanne Maroney, who handles consumer complaints for a branch of the Better Business Bureau, says, "The success of advertising and our failure to defend ourselves against it is the result of this 'I'm not taken in' attitude. Too many people don't realize that ad companies spend millions of dollars a year researching people's deepest motivations so they can persuade them without having them realize that they *are* being persuaded."

What motivational research reveals about people's buying habits is often fascinating. For example, a long time ago, Johnson & Johnson came out with a first aid cream that didn't sting when applied to an open cut. Proud to be first to market this new formula, the company executives expected profits to soar. But the cream didn't sell. "Why not?" the Johnson people wondered. Well, one of their motivational studies showed that people just don't feel a medication is really effective unless it hurts a little. Things that are "good" for you have to make you suffer, the reasoning goes. So Johnson & Johnson put a little alcohol back into their cream, which restored the nip, and sales went right back up. Pharmaceutical companies have been smarter ever since. The latest Listerine commercials, for example, appeal directly to this masochistic quirk of human nature. "It tastes *terrible*," grimaces one man after gargling with Listerine, "but it sure works!" The craftiness of ads like this led scholar Henryk Skolimowki to remark, "We think that language is a tool, a device that we use to communicate. We do indeed use it. But language also uses *us*—by shaping our desires and feelings, by manipulating our buying habits.''

Picture, if you will, the following scene: You're in your local supermarket, doing your shopping for the week. You need some toothpaste, so you go to the pharmacy section. You start to reach for your usual brand, Crest, but then you stop yourself. Maybe you should try something different? Something that would taste, oh, *better* somehow. There's the pile of Aim toothpaste all lined up next to the Crest. *That* looks good, you decide, and throw a tube into your shopping basket. You think you've made a perfectly rational choice, based on your own personal preferences and desires? Yes?

Careful.

Most probably you've fallen victim to the adman's hype. *Why* did you decide to change brands at this particular time? Because you were dissatisfied with your old brand? Probably not. Chances are that Crest was getting your teeth as white and clean and cavity-free as they'll ever be. And you must like the taste, to have used it all these years. Besides, as long as a toothpaste doesn't taste like kerosene, how important is taste? Toothpaste is something you have in your mouth for only thirty seconds or so a day.

So why did you switch rather than fight? Because after hours and hours of watching Aim commercials and being told that "Aim tastes better," you finally caved in. Consciously or subconsciously, you came to believe it: "Aim tastes better."

Now ask yourself: "Better than what? Better than an oatmeal cookie? Better than day-old bacon fat? Better than garden fertilizer?" Because that could be what the adman is comparing Aim to. Of course, he wants you to think Aim tastes better than the other toothpastes on the market. But that's not what he *said*; he said, "Aim tastes better"—and that's all. And *you* bought it. You were suckered by one of the oldest, most effective of all the adman's bag of tricks—the dangling comparative. (Any statement that suggests that a product is superior and doesn't say what it is superior *to* is a dangling comparative: "Firestone Radial Tires stop 25% faster." Faster than what? A doughnut?) What is worse, you're not even aware of how you were influenced by the ad; you think you're buying Aim just because you feel like it. But it was the adman who *made* you feel that way.

"Why are so many mothers of cavity-prone children switching to Aim?" the ad continues. A wonderful example of the logical fallacy known as begging the question—meaning that the question includes a premise that has not been proven. *Why* are so many mothers of cavity-prone children switching to Aim? Who ever said that mothers *were* switching to Aim? How do we know this is true? Can it be proven? Of course, it doesn't really make any difference whether it can or not, because what people remember is what has been suggested. As the shoeshine boy said, explaining why he got more customers than any of his rivals, "I give them the same old shoeshine, but I snap the rag a lot!"

The dangling comparative and begging the question are tricks well known to that experienced wordsmith, the adman. In fact, the slippery language tactics used by admen are so common that they have even been given their own name—weasel words.

So what is a weasel word? First of all, let's remember what a weasel is. *Webster's New World Dictionary* defines it as "a cunning, agile, flesh-eating mammal that feeds on rats, mice, eggs, etc." Not exactly the kind of fellow you'd invite home to meet dear old mom. His namesake, the weasel word, is hardly more attractive. A weasel word is a word used to *suggest* or *imply* something that the adman cannot actually come right out and say. After all, outright lies in advertising are forbidden by law, and you cannot make a statement in an ad that is baldly untrue without having the Federal Trade Commission admonish you. So the adman cannot lie; he can only deceive. Appearances may be deceiving, but in the world of commercial advertising, weasel words are even more deceiving. Weasel words make you hear things that aren't being said and thereby make you believe things that simply aren't true. For example, in the Aim commercial, you are led to believe that the makers of Aim toothpaste are making two specific claims about their product: (1) that Aim tastes better than the other leading toothpastes on the market, and (2) that many people are switching to Aim because of its superiority over the other brands. In fact, neither of these statements is made by the ad, though each is certainly implied, and if you took the company to court to protest that these claims aren't true, you wouldn't have a legal leg to stand on. The company could point out that neither of these claims was ever made. Is it their fault if you reach false conclusions about the claims in the ad? This is Madison Avenue's Catch-22.

See how good you are at detecting the weasel in the following statement:

> Three out of four doctors recommend the major ingredient in Anacin for the relief of headache pain.

Did you catch the weasel hiding in the undergrowth? It's the phrase "the major ingredient." What *is* this major ingredient? Some revolutionary new painkiller? A secret concoction available only to those wise enough to buy Anacin? Not at all. The "major ingredient" in Anacin is aspirin. Plain, unadulterated, inexpensive aspirin, available in economy bottles that cost less than half as much as Anacin. *Of course* three out of four doctors recommend aspirin. This doesn't mean that three out of four doctors recommend *Anacin*. But the implication hangs over the statement like a thick fog. Who can blame the unwary listener who assumes that this is what is being said? But it would be equally fair to say that poisoned orange juice has a major ingredient that doctors recommend—orange juice!

Try another one on for size:

If Nescafé can please the whole wide world, it can sure please you.

This time you were probably alert to the rustling in the under-growth, and perhaps you bagged the game—as wet-nosed, wiggly, and whopping a weasel as ever trod the pages of advertising copy. It is, of course, the little word "if." "If Nescafé can please the whole wide world . . ." Notice that they don't say that Nescafé *does* please the whole wide world, just that *if* it did then it could be expected to "please" you too. Fine. *If* I were queen, my husband would be king. And if weasels were elephants, ivory would be cheaper. The possibilities of "if" are endless. And iffy.

Beginning to feel the thrill of excitement that accompanies the hunt? Good. Let's see if we can bag another weasel:

This sneaker was washed twice in Tide. (Accompanied by a picture of a very dirty sneaker.) This sneaker was washed once the Dynamo Way. (Accompanied by a picture of a spanking-clean sneaker.)

It's there, all right. The weasel is "the Dynamo Way." The question you should ask yourself is, "Why do they say that one sneaker was washed the *Dynamo Way* and not just in *Dynamo?*" After all, they say the dirty sneaker was washed *in Tide.* What *is* the Dynamo Way to wash sneakers? Maybe it means running that sneaker through the washer fourteen times. Or maybe it means adding twice as much detergent as you ordinarily would. Or hiring ten washerwomen to scrub that sneaker with Dynamo for three days. Or, horrid thought, maybe the Dynamo sneaker wasn't dirty in the first place?

If you love cars, here's an interesting weasel:

Lowest sticker price in America.

The weasel here is "sticker." The price on the sticker isn't necessarily the final going price of the car—not by a long shot.

There are all kinds of hidden costs—for "options" like air conditioning or a radio, for "preparation" and "transportation" costs, and so on. How many of these extra costs are listed on the sticker is really up to the dealer. Volkswagen, for example, recently introduced a new model with a very low sticker price—which didn't include, among other thing, carpeting or floor mats. Without them, the interior looked like the inside of a tank. If the car the dealer was advertising was really the cheapest car you could buy, why didn't the ad say, "Lowest *price* in America"? Good question. If they were to rephrase the ad to read, "Other manufacturers may sell their cars cheaper, but nobody *advertises* a cheaper price than we do," would that thrill you? Not likely.

Here's a particularly subtle weasel for you to try your bow and arrow on:

Geritol has twice the iron of any ordinary supplement. It's a very important mineral.

The weasel is a bit tougher to spot because it's hiding under an innocent-looking pronoun—"it." "It" here refers to the iron, not the Geritol. Look at that sentence structure again. Wouldn't a lot of listeners *assume* that Geritol is the important mineral? The indefinite antecedent is the very lifeblood of the weasel. If you're reminded of the magician's trick of distracting your eye from what is really going on, you're beginning to catch on.

By now you may be able to recognize a weasel at first sight:

Introducing New Ground Sanka. We think it's twice as good.

Ah, the familiar features of the dangling comparative! The Sanka people could be saying New Ground Sanka is twice as good as an unprocessed coffee bean. If you wanted to hold them to account, you might point out that twice zero is still zero, or (if you wanted to be even stricter) that twice as good as rotten is still pretty bad.

Who's that skulking around the corner? Ah, hah, another weasel:

Our tobacco is cured for up to eight long, lazy weeks.

Do you think this means that their tobacco is cured for eight weeks? It isn't. It's cured for *up to* eight weeks. That's all the difference in the world. To back up this statement, all they have to do is cure *one* batch of tobacco for eight weeks, then cure all the rest for ten days, or one day, or even one hour. And while we're at it, what on earth is a "long" week, anyway? The amount of time it takes a family of four to consume a "jumbo" quart of milk, perhaps? Is a "lazy" week equal to three months? Four? Do eight lazy weeks still have fifty-six days? Or is the calendar too lazy to count?

I've saved a particularly sneaky weasel for the last, so you could have a good shot at it!

No plain antacid has the Di-Gel difference.

The adman obviously couldn't think of anything to say about the product that would make anyone want to buy it, so he used the product name itself to suggest that the product is somehow different or special. He avoids telling us—and one must think he does so deliberately—what the Di-Gel difference is. Di-Gel is different because it *is* Di-Gel, we are left to assume. "No plain antacid has the Di-Gel difference" because no other product is named Di-Gel or comes in a Di-Gel box. In other words, "No plain antacid is named Di-Gel," or, in short, "Di-Gel is Di-Gel." A classic instance of a dog chasing its own tail.

Di-Gel is not the only product to use this weasel:

Only Hershey bars have Hershey's chocolate.
If it doesn't say Q-tips, then it isn't Q-tips swabs.

This is about as significant as saying, "I am I," or "I am myself," or "I am me," or, "No one but me has my particular identity." The adman would refine this to, "Only I have the special 'me' ingredient."

You can continue playing "find the weasel" whenever you like simply by turning on the TV or picking up a magazine. But even if you get to be the world expert at detecting weasel words, you still will not be safe, because there are lots of other ways an adman can use words to snare you.

A friend of mine, a very intelligent woman, prides herself on her relative immunity to advertising propaganda. I was having lunch with her at one of our favorite greasy spoon places a few weeks ago. After we had finished the chiliburgers, and were just beginning, with a twinge of anxiety and regret, to reflect on the pieces of ground-up insect we had probably ingested along with them, I saw her pull out a package of Certs and take one. In the course of researching this chapter, I got into the annoying habit of asking friends *why* they bought a particular product. So I asked, "Why do you buy Certs instead of, say, Dynamint—or even just plain Life Savers?"

Without hesitation, she replied, "Because Certs have retsyn."

"And what is retsyn?"

Here she hesitated. "Why, it's the scientific ingredient that they put in to help freshen your breath. It's what makes Certs stronger than regular Life Savers."

"How does it work?" I asked.

"Oh, I don't know—kills germs or something."

Well, we looked at the Certs package, and there in tiny print was the answer to what retsyn is—vegetable oil!

The plain fact is that there is an irresistible appeal, in this modern technological age, for anything that sounds scientific. What all admen are looking for is the "wienie"—the angle, the gimmick, the something that need not be different as long as it sounds different. Science has become their savior. Copywriters earnestly study chemical laboratory analyses in search of the elusive "wienie"—the more exotic-sounding and incomprehensible the better.

Sometimes something as simple as a single letter can make all the difference. In 1895, an epochal event occurred: the discovery of the X ray. What X rays did for medicine is nothing compared to what they did for language. The discovery of X rays liberated the *X*. Today, any product with an *X* in its name is almost guaranteed to be regarded as technologically advanced. Thus, we have things like Pyrex, the glass dishware that can be placed directly on the burner of a stove without breaking. Actually, it is just tempered glass, easily manufactured, and not exactly a scientific breakthrough on the magnitude of, say, the discovery of fire or the wheel. (If our cave-dwelling ancestors had been obliged to market these items, we would be calling them firex or wheelex.) But the name suggests that Pyrex is in the vanguard of modern technology, the end result of extensive laboratory testing and development. Would you really be as attracted to Pyrex if it were called "High Heat" or "Sturdiglas" or "Duraware"?

And what about all the other products with *X* in their names? Timex watches, for example? That *X* ending assures you *this* watch will keep time reliably, accurately, *scientifically?* That's why the manufacturers didn't call their product "Tim*er*" watches instead. Then there's Xerox copying machines, whose creators must have been canny men, for they foresaw the great future of the *X*, and endowed their product with *two* of them!

Why is the twenty-fourth letter of the alphabet such a magical aid in marketing? Exxon, perhaps the only word with two consecutive *X*s, is a computer-generated trademark. The *X* seems to be connected with science, math, and computers in most people's minds. W. Klingshirm, a professor at Holy Cross College, has come up with a theory to explain the association between *X* and computers: "Composed of two clean, perpendicular diagonals, the X is binary, like computer language, and it sounds like a clicking terminal. Its bilateral

and radical symmetry give it a balanced, geometric flavor."
Dr. Klingshirm may never be asked to write copy for a cosmetic ad, but his point is still well taken. The X is a symbol of our modern computer age.

Including X in the tradename isn't the only way an adman suggests that his product is truly modern and scientific. The letters of the alphabet can be combined endlessly to suggest that a product is truly modern and/or scientific. Gasoline additives provide an example of what a clever marketing man can do with a little time and a feel for acronyms. There's Esso, with HTA. What is HTA? It could be pink lemonade for all we know. But *HTA* sounds like a mysterious formula, and that must be enough to convince some of us that we should buy Esso gasoline. Not to be outdone, Esso's competitors decided to advertise their "scientific" additives, too. The gas companies are waging a war of gasoline additives that has begun to sound like a convention of creatures from outer space: Arkkoa with Ethylmate, Chevron with F-310, etc. Do we know what these mystery formulas are? Or why they're used? Or what they *do* for our cars? No.

Our modern reverence for all things scientific isn't the only quirk that an adman can capitalize on to sell a product. Any good copywriter knows lots of useful buzz words that will convince an unwary consumer to buy. A "buzz word" is a word that is "in," a word that is used so often that it sets up a sort of humming in the brain that deafens you to the questions of your rational mind. Imagine, for example, a cosmetics counter in an exclusive department store. A pretty young girl approaches, looking for a skin care lotion. There is an unbelievable array before her—bottles, tubes, jars, creams, unguents, lotions, powders, in every possible color and fragrance. Which shall she choose? she wonders. Should she buy the Peach cleansing cream? Or would the Cucumber be better? That Lemon Pore lotion looks so cool and inviting, but she can't ignore the Apricot Moisturizing Magic and the Avocado shampoo, which look (literally) appetizing. Oh, my, it's just *so* hard to decide between all these taste-tantalizing delights. And think of their versatility! Even if these items do nothing for her skin, they can provide enough food for a month.

Why the enormous assortment of incredible edibles? Because, as every adman worth his salt and pepper knows, fruits are "in." Fruit names are the biggest buzz words of today. Words like "lemon" and "strawberry" and "peach" have such strong reverberations that they have been known to numb certain regions of the cerebral cortex, creating an aphasia that prevents the consumer from asking, "What's so great about peaches in a moisturizing cream?" True, peaches have nice soft skins and are lovely to touch, but that doesn't mean these qualities can "rub off" on you. After all the decades of experimentation by dermatologists, it seems unlikely that we can't come up with anything better for the skin than the lowly peach. It's even harder to see the appeal of a product like "Peach Thrill," a dishwashing soap. What can peaches possibly do to make your dishes cleaner or shinier? If you wouldn't squeeze a peach over your dishes to make them clean, why pay more for a soap with peaches in it?

Which doesn't take into account the fact that most products using the "fruit gimmick" don't even have real fruit in them. Peaches and lemons are far too expensive to be included in most products, so the manufacturers use chemicals that have the same aroma as the fruit. Then they use artificial colors to make the product the same color as the fruit. In the world of the weasel, you must never make the mistake of thinking that a product described as "lemony" or "lemon-refreshed" or "lemon-active" has ever gotten within ten yards of a real lemon. You're just paying more for a scented chemical, which likely as not has no useful function other than to get you to buy the product.

The sad fact is that there is no end to this fruit madness in sight. Fruits are already exploding into new product areas. Witness "lemon-refreshed" Mr. Clean, and lemon-scented deodorant powder. To what far-out regions of an adman's imagination will this fad take us? Will we soon have Squirt, the grapefruit-refreshed laundry detergent? Pom-Pom, the pomegranate throat gargle? Percy, the persimmon-based cure for athlete's foot? How about orange-laced shoe polish? Prune-powered toilet bowl cleaner?

The current hoopla over fruits is part of the general public fascination with all things natural. And the word "natural" is one of the biggest buzz words of all. A 1977 survey of consumer opinion revealed that most consumers think "natural" products are better because they are pure, free of additives or chemicals, and healthful. Not so. Witness the plague of "natural" cereals (containing refined and certainly *un*healthful sugars), "naturally flavored" soft drinks (made with acetic acid, artificial color, and sodium benzoate), and "natural" hair-colorings (a concept that must have been dreamed up by the same genius who gave us "authentic replica"). It's come to the point where "natural" doesn't mean anything anymore. Take, for example, Rheingold, the "natural" beer. What does "natural" mean here? That it is made out of natural things like water, hops, malt, etc., presumably. But aren't *all* beers made out of these things? Coors isn't made of plastic or cotton polyester. "Natural" here means precisely nothing, but as a buzz word it's very successful. A vice-president of the advertising firm that handles the Rheingold account says, "The initial reaction to the ad is just fantastic. We're going great guns right now." Apparently, some consumers are switching to Rheingold beer because they believe that it's a more natural beer than the others on the market. Buzz, buzz.

The adman has a tough job. He's got to sell a product that often is no better than or different from hundreds of others, yet he must make it *seem* better or different. Suppose a company that makes little cat yummies comes to Young & Rubicam (one of the big Madison Avenue ad agencies) with its account. The company wants Young & Rubicam to make its cat yummies a household word. Now, the copywriters at Young

& Rubicam know that eighty million American cats are not eagerly awaiting the day they can get their yummies. There's not much the copywriters can do about that. They can hardly suggest that the company shut down the plant and start selling something useful, like raisins. No, instead they must find a way to convince the American consumer (it's hard to reason with the cats) that these cat yummies are vital to the health and well-being of said cats, that cats may in fact leave home if they do not get these yummies, that the entire family structure may break apart—Dad will be haggard and anxious, Mom will become a grumpy nag, kids will leave home—IF THESE CATS DON'T GET THEIR YUMMIES!

How can the hardworking copywriters at Young & Rubicam accomplish this miracle? Partly by using the techniques we've already talked about. First, they'll give the product a name that capitalizes on the national reverence for science: Formula *280X*. Then they'll add an appeal to the fruit fad crowd—"Tangerine Formula 280X: the *natural* food for your cat." Finally, they'll throw in some weasel words to convince us of the yummies' importance to the well-being of cats everywhere: "Three out of four doctors recommend the major ingredient in our Tangerine Formula 280X as part of your pet's everyday nutritional needs." (The major ingredient is water.)

In the end, though, what will *sell* the product is the emotional pitch. The number one rule of admen is: If you're stuck with a parity product (one that is exactly the same—or maybe worse—than the competing products on the market), don't talk about the product itself; talk about the person who is buying the product. Enter the apotheosis of the adman's creed: the image ad.

The image ad is so-called because it sells a desirable image of the buyer rather than of the product. Our Y & R copywriters, searching for a way to sell their client's cat yummies (now rechristened Tangerine Formula 280X), decide a family image would probably work best: Mom and Dad in a cozy (not too luxurious) family room, looking on fondly as their two adorable kids (one girl and one boy) feed the kitties (two black and two white) who devour the yummies ravenously (they haven't been fed for two days).

Dad says, "Gee, Mom, those cats sure love that new Tangerine Formula 280X."

Mom smiles knowingly. "Of course they do. Tangerine Formula 280X is delicious." No one inquires as to how she has discovered this. "And they're so good for them, too. (Picture cuts away to shot of a laboratory test tube as Mom continues:) Each yummie portion of Tangerine Formula 280X has been scientifically tested in a special animal testing center in Biloxi. The results are startling: Three out of four doctors recommend the major ingredient in Tangerine Formula 280X as a necessary part of a cat's nutritional needs."

Son: "Gee, Mom, I didn't know that."

Dad: "Gee. Aren't we lucky to have such a smart Mom?" (Kisses wife.)

Daughter: "Gee, we sure are!"

Mom, smiling and holding up a box of cat yummies: "Tangerine Formula 280X. The *natural* food for your cat." (Music swells.)

And there you have it. A pinch of buzz words, a dollop of weasels to spice up a generous serving of image appeal. Bubble, bubble, toil and trouble, admen earn and profits double.

Many products are sold almost exclusively by image, without the need to rely on weasel or buzz words. Usually image ads are used for parity products, which are all pretty much alike, so there's nothing that can be said (legally) to convince the buyer that one brand is better than another.

Cigarettes are the best example of products sold by image appeal. Some years back, Virginia Slims cigarettes exploded onto the market with their "You've come a long way, baby" ad. You'll notice that the ad makes no pretense of discussing the cigarette itself. It talks about how confined women were in the past ("Back in Victorian Days, a woman decorated her parlor with a lot of knickknacks and clutter because . . . it was harder for her husband to see her if she wanted to sneak a cigarette") and how liberated they are now (a picture of a glamorous woman, usually scantily clad, with a cigarette dangling saucily from her lips). That's all. No mention of the cigarette itself—how it compares to other brands in price, quality, or taste. Just the "liberated woman" image (one that is offensive to many women, who detect the patronizing note in being called "baby"). Sales skyrocketed.

Because of the success of the Virginia Slims campaign, other firms rushed to get in on the "liberated woman" image. In an ad for Fantastik spray cleaner, a housewife says, "Don't call me a housewife; I'm not married to my house." However, this image is as hollow as the Virginia Slims appeal. No one calls the "Fantastik" housewife "baby," but it turns out that this supposedly liberated character only wants more time to fill her customary woman's role—looking after hubby and kids. She just doesn't want to be *called* "housewife." Hardly the stuff of which revolutions are made. Still, the "Don't call me a housewife" line has a powerful appeal.

Image appeals to women are so successful that there is now an entire firm dedicated to it—the Advertising to Women agency, founded and directed by Lois Geraci Ernst. Ms. Ernst herself has created one of the most successful image ads of the 70s—for a new perfume called Aviance. The ad shows a woman dressed in drab housewife garb—shapeless apron and scarf tied around the head—mopping the kitchen floor. Suddenly, she throws down the mop, whips off the apron and scarf, and reveals a sexy dress underneath. She puts on a bit of lipstick, and, natch, some Aviance perfume, and presto! She's a desirable, sexy woman off to have an "Aviance Night." (There's no doubt about what that is when you see the look on her handsome escort's face as he greets her at the door. She's not going to need her mop tonight— unless it's for something kinky!) Again, remember that the ad says absolutely nothing about the product or why we should buy it. And apparently, who cares? Aviance sales are booming.

"Liberated woman" isn't the only successful image going around. The old "upper crust" image is still effective. Dewar's White Label runs an ad which "profiles" various people. One profile is of a female nuclear physicist, one a successful black businesswoman. (All Dewar's people are superior, sophisticated characters.) The ad lets us in on their taste in books (*The Pathos of Power* by Kenneth Clark) and on their hobbies (collecting contemporary art), and never says a word about the whiskey. Employing a similar approach, the Great Books series published by the Encyclopaedia Britannica announces that its product is for "People who are not ashamed of having brains," and goes on to announce to anyone who happens to be reading: "You were probably born with a bigger share of intelligence than most of your fellow men . . . and taught how to use it. And you appreciate it. You aren't ashamed of having brains. You enjoy using them." Apparently the criterion for having this superior cranial capacity is your ability to read the ad.

Big corporations try to avoid the "upper crust" image, preferring a "just one of the folks" appeal. Martin Marietta, for example, is a giant conglomerate that markets chemicals, cement, and aluminum, among other things. Its latest ad shows a gray-haired, motherly looking woman in a white apron smiling benevolently out at the reader. The copy reads:

> Tucked into an old Latin American neighborhood not far from downtown Detroit, is Aliette's Bakery. It is a restaurant within a bakery. Seven tables. Run by a lady who will tell you to eat your onion soup because it is good for your health and energy. . . .
>
> She works a sixteen-hour day, doing almost everything herself. Shopping for meat, filleting a 60-pound side of veal, cooking sauces, rolling out pastry, waiting on tables, cleaning up.

"At night I'm so tired I'm afraid to sit down because I won't get up again and I still have more to do." But that's all right. The smile on your face when you're eating her seven-layer chocolate cake makes it all worthwhile. . . .

You're wondering what connection Aliette and her bakery have to Martin Marietta Chemical Corporation? Even the ad writers for Martin Marietta must have pondered that one for a while—but they dredged up a connection in the end:

We're Martin Marietta Corporation. We want everyone to know about people who do their jobs in an excellent way. The things we make are so much a part of America that we have an interest in making America better for everyone.

Aliette, *merci.*

A bit strained, perhaps, but the message is clear: Martin Marietta isn't a big, impersonal corporate conglomerate; no, it's a warm, caring, *gemütlich* person who wants nothing more than to "make America better for everyone"—by putting a seven-layer cake on every table, presumably.

The most famous—and admired—image campaign of the century is the one for Marlboro cigarettes. Many years ago, Marlboro was a "woman's cigarette" and dying fast, when the manufacturers decided something had to be done,. They hired an ad agency to give their product a new image. The copywriters proposed a simple and dramatic change: Marlboro would do better as a *man's* cigarette. They came up with the idea of the "Marlboro Man"—a rough, tough, outdoors type who sported a tattoo on his muscular arm. The guy didn't have to appear really *sexy,* because his appeal wasn't for women—just tough, silent, strong—a man's man. After a few months of advertising its new image, Marlboro began to prosper. Today, Marlboro is still one of the best-selling cigarettes on the market, but the image has been modified somewhat to emphasize the great outdoors—showing Mr. Masculinity on a horse in the distance (whether or not he still has the tattoo, only his horse knows). The miraculous and almost overnight success of this change in image is one of the seven wonders of the advertising world. A senior ad exec at one of the big New York ad agencies says, "Marlboro? A sensational ad campaign—really, an historic one, since so many other accounts have now jumped on the 'great outdoors' bandwagon. Mention the name Marlboro around here and people genuflect." His admiration is justified. Overnight, Marlboro ceased to be a cigarette for women and became a cigarette for men, although nothing about the product itself was changed. Hail, the power of the image maker!

Despite the manifest effectiveness of advertising, many of us persist in thinking that we are immune from its appeal. A friend of mine certainly feels that way. He ridicules "those suckers" who fall for an image ad. "I'm not stupid enough to be taken in," he insists. "When I buy something, it's because it's a quality product, not because I've been influenced by some ad. When I buy a cigarette, it's because it has the best taste. After all, you can't smoke an image!" What's his brand of cigarettes, you wonder? Winston. And what's the Winston ad, you ask? Good question. The Winston ad pictures a dark, handsome guy, who looks very independent, saying, "Some people smoke a brand for its image. I don't. You can't taste image. I smoke for taste. I smoke Winston." This is the ultimate image ad—the image of a person who doesn't fall for an image!

So there you are. No one is entirely safe from the long arm of the adman. And we are everywhere surrounded by his creations—on TV, in magazines, in buses and subways, in our favorite restaurants, and on our highways. Words are even being used to attack us in our most private moments, as ads begin to appear on the inside of toilet booths and on toilet paper dispensers. Doubtless, some enterprising soul will soon be selling us the end products of such meditative interludes. Here, then, with weasel words intact, is what the adman might do when confronted with the problem of how to market human excrement:

> Announcing a new and different approach to home gardening. Compoo, a 100% scientifically tested and proven completely effective organic garden nutrient. Guaranteed, completely biodegradable components have been naturally processed up to 48 hours. Have more verdant greenery both indoors and out in half the time! It's amazingly easy to handle; its smooth pliable texture is easily worked into the soil and will not harm skin like harsh chemicals. Preferred by 9 out of 10 successful gardeners, Compoo's secret ingredients will make your lawn the envy of your neighborhood.
>
> Compoo is available in a variety of earth-tone colors and comes packaged in a lovely, discreet, reclosable decorator sack, which will be the focal point of your garden shed. Or you may prefer the handsome reusable crock. Gardeners in the know are switching to Compoo. Shouldn't you? Ask for it where quality garden products are sold.

5

Color Me a Word

A very great part of the mischiefs that vex this world arises from words.

Edmund Burke

While Joan Anderson, American, was touring Berlin with her boyfriend, German-born Hans Fritsch, he got into an argument with the cabdriver about the fare. The cabbie was loud and obnoxious and Hans's reasonableness only seemed to make him more angry. Finally, he swung around to face Hans and spat out the word *"Schweinhund!"* Though normally calm and easygoing, Hans turned red with fury and would have struck the cabby if Joan had not intervened. Enraged, he threw some money at the cabby and stalked off. Later at dinner, Joan asked Hans to explain his violent response to the word the driver used.

"You mean *Schweinhund?*" asked Hans.

"Yes."

"Oh, it's a serious insult, a disgusting, tasteless remark that only a lowlife like that fellow would make."

"So what does it *mean?*" persisted Joan.

"Oh, well, it means . . . well, I guess it really means . . . 'pig dog.' "

"Pig dog?" Joan repeated in disbelief. "You mean that's

111

the unspeakably insulting thing he said to you? Why, that's ridiculous! It . . . it's laughable. Why ever did you become so upset about it?''

At a loss to explain his reaction, Hans shrugged and said, "Well, it loses something in the translation.''

Certain phrases, words, ideas do lose in translation from one language to another. For example, our word "executive" translates into German as "*leitende Mann*" or "leading man,'' a phrase which seems to us to belong more to the theater than to the world of business. In Spanish, the same word translates as "*director de empresas*" or "director of enterprises,'' a phrase that captures the connection with business more successfully, but still lacks the range of meaning we attach to our word "executive" (witness our "executive look,'' "executive suite,'' "executive phone'').

The same problem occurs in reverse with words like "*Schweinhund*,'' whose full meaning never survives the sea change from German to English. Imagine yourself in Germany, visiting with some distant cousins who speak no English. One day, sitting out on the back porch with your cousins, you see the family who lives across the way on their back lawn. It's a lovely scene: the father and two young boys are chasing around after a ball, making a terrible racket, while the mother, smiling, watches them. Your cousin says, "*Gumütlichkeit, ja?*'' In your trusty English/German, German/English dictionary, this means "easygoing disposition,'' so you figure your cousin may be referring to the mother, who is relaxed and smiling while her family reduces her backyard to rubble. However, "*Gemütlichkeit*'' has another listed meaning: "cheerfulness, happiness.'' That might refer to the mother, too, of course, but then again, it *could* refer to the players. Well, it doesn't really matter, it's got *something* to do with being happy, and you're about to put away the pocket dictionary when you spot another translation: "freedom from worry about money.'' So maybe that's what your cousin is commenting on, not the family's simple enjoyment of a game, but

on their financial status. Unfortunately, this idea is under-
mined by the following definition, "sentiment," which is followed by still *more* definitions, including "sanguineness,"
"good-naturedness," and "adorableness." So about all you
can get out of your cousin's remark is that he is saying *something* nice about the family and the way they live.

The problems of translation are further complicated by the
fact that in German every noun has a gender—that is, it is
either male or female or neuter. So, when you cast a German
sentence into English, you inevitably lose the gender of the
noun. Mark Twain, a man with an acute eye for absurdity, ridicules the German system of noun genders in his famous essay "The Awful German Language":

> . . . In German, a young lady has no sex, while a tur-
> nip has. Think what overwrought reverence that
> shows for the turnip, and what callous disrespect for
> the girl. See how it looks in print—I translate this from
> a conversation in one of the best of the German Sun-
> day-school books:
> Gretchen—Wilhelm, where is the turnip?
> Wilhelm—She has gone to the kitchen.
> Gretchen—Where is the accomplished and
>   beautiful English maiden?
> Wilhelm—It has gone to the opera.

And this is just the beginning of the whimsicality of German
genders:

> . . . a tree is male, its buds are female, its leaves are
> neuter; horses are sexless, dogs are male, cats are fe-
> male—tomcats included, of course; a person's mouth,
> neck, bosom, elbows, fingers, nails, feet and body are
> of the male sex, and his head is male or neuter accord-
> ing to the word selected to signify it, and not according
> to the sex of the individual who wears it—for in Ger-
> many, all the women wear either male heads or sexless
> ones; a person's nose, lips, shoulders, breast, hands

and toes are of the female sex; and his hair, ears, eyes, chin, legs, knees, heart and conscience haven't any sex at all. . . .

In the German, it is true that by some oversight of the inventor of the language, a Woman is female, but a Wife (weib) is not—which is unfortunate. A wife, here, has no sex; she is neuter; so, according to the grammar, a fish is *he*, his scales are *she*, but a fishwife is neither. . . .

Finally, Twain puts all this together to show you how a German story would look if properly translated into the English—with all genders intact:

TALE OF THE FISHWIFE AND ITS SAD FATE

It is a bleak day. Hear the Rain, how he pours, and the Hail, how he rattles; and see the Snow, how he drifts along, and oh, the Mud, how deep he is! Ah, the poor Fishwife, it is stuck fast in the Mire; it has dropped its Basket of Fishes; and its Hands have been cut by the Scales as it seized some of the falling Creatures; and one Scale has even got into its Eye, and it cannot get her out. It opens its Mouth to cry for Help; but if any Sound comes out of him, alas, he is drowned by the raging of the Storm. And now a Tomcat has got one of the Fishes and she will surely escape with him. No, she bites off a Fin, she holds her in her Mouth—will she swallow her? No, the Fishwife's brave Mother-dog deserts his puppies and rescues the Fin—which he eats, himself, as his Reward. O, horror, the Lightning has struck the Fish-basket; he sets him on Fire; see the Flame, how she licks the doomed Utensil with her red and angry Tongue; now she attacks the helpless Fishwife's Foot—she burns him up, all but the big Toe, and even *she* is partly consumed; and still she spreads, still she waves her fiery Tongues; she attacks the Fishwife's Leg and destroys *it*; she attacks its Hand and destroys *her*; she attacks its poor, worn Garment and destroys *her* also; she attacks its Body and consumes *him*; she wreathes herself about its Breast, and in a Moment *she* is a Cinder; now she reaches its Heart and *it* is consumed; next about its Neck—*he* goes; now its Chin—it goes; now its Nose—*she* goes. In another Moment, except Help come, the Fishwife will be no more. Time passes—is there none to succor and save? Yes! Joy! Joy! With flying Feet, the she-Englishwoman comes! But alas, the generous she-female is too late. Where now is the fated Fishwife? It has ceased from its Sufferings, it has gone to a better Land; all that is left of it for its loved ones to lament over is this poor smoldering Ash-heap. Ah, woeful, woeful Ash-heap! Let us take him up tenderly, reverently, upon the lowly Shovel, and bear him to his long Rest, with the Prayer that when he rises again it will be in a Realm where he will have one, good, square, responsible Sex, and have it all to himself, instead of having a mangy lot of assorted Sexes scattered all over him in Spots.[1]

Many people think that translation is simply a matter of substituting a word in one language for a word in another, but this is not the case. Foreign language words often mean something quite different from what they appear to. A United States Army chaplain serving in France once blessed a French soldier with the words "*Que Dieu vous préserve,*" which would logically seem to mean "May God préserve you." Unfortunately, in French, "*préserver*" means "to pickle." And a young girl visiting Spain with her mother couldn't understand why everyone burst out laughing when she apologized for accidentally spilling the contents of her purse on the hotel lobby floor. "*Estoy embarazada,*" she had said, meaning that she felt embarrassed. "*Embarazada,*" unhappily, also means "pregnant" in Spanish. Even more embarrassingly pregnant with meaning is a translation discovered by W. H. Auden in a phrase book written by a well-meaning Italian to help promote understanding between British and Italian troops after World War II. He translated the Italian phrase *"Posse presentate il conte"* ("Allow me to present the count") as "Meet the cunt."

Amusing examples of fractured English translations are legion. Linguist Clyde Kluckhohn once asked a Japanese friend to translate into English the phrase in the Japanese Constitution that is the equivalent of our "life, liberty, and the pursuit of happiness." It emerged in English as "license to commit lustful pleasure." On another occasion, Kluckhohn had the phrase "Genevieve suspended for prank" translated from English to Russian and then back again to English. It came out, "Genevieve hanged for juvenile delinquency." Recently, there's the example of the unfortunate Steven Seymour, who botched his translation of President Carter's official address to the Polish people. When Carter spoke of "departing" Washington to pay a state visit to Poland, Seymour rendered it as "abandoning" the U.S. When Carter referred to the Polish people's "hopes" for the future, Seymour's translation called it the Polish people's "lusts."

With all the possibilities for error, we should pity the poor men and women working as translators at the UN who have to translate important ideas instantaneously and as accurately as possible. Subtle distinctions may make the difference between peaceful coexistence and war. Rudolf Flesch, who has researched some of the problems of those who drew up the UN charter, says,

> When the UN charter was written, Latin Americans protested that the phrase *sovereign equality* didn't mean a thing to them; they preferred *personality of states*, a phrase meaningless to everyone else. The French, it turned out, had no word for *trusteeship*, the Chinese had trouble in translating *steering committee*, the Spanish-speaking members couldn't express the difference between *chairman* and *president*.[2]

Apparently, the charter committee was able to iron out

these linguistic wrinkles, and today the UN goes on with trusteeships and steering committees that may not be called the same things by all the member countries. Which just proves that if you work at it hard enough, you can usually manage to communicate a major idea from one language to another. But the subtleties don't usually survive the process of translation. Luckily, for everyday purposes, subtleties aren't important. Take this translation of Tokyo traffic regulations:

> When a passenger of the foot heave in sight, tootle the horn, trumpet at him melodiously at first, but if he still obstacles your passage, tootle him with vigor, express by mouth the warning Hi, hi! Beware the wandering horse that he shall not take fright as you pass him by. Do not explode the exhaust box at him. Go soothingly by. Give big space to the festive dog that shall sport in the roadway. Go soothingly in the grease-mud as there lurks the skid-demon. Avoid the tanglement of the dog with your wheel spokes. Press the braking of the foot as you roll round the corner to save collapse and tie-up.[3]

Although the translation might be said to lack certain subtleties of English speech, the central meaning is clear enough, and any American tourist who skids off the road will know it's his own damn fault for imprudently refusing to take fair warning and go soothingly through the grease-mud.

It's in translations of literary works, which depend so much for their effect on subtler shadings of meaning and emotion, that the real problems of translation show up. Here, for example, is a translation of a famous Japanese haiku (a three-line, seventeen-syllable minipoem):

> By morning glories
> I have had my well-bucket captured
> and I borrow my water.

This version leans so heavily toward the cryptic, it's practically horizontal. A different translation makes the idea somewhat clearer:

> All round the rope a morning-glory clings
> How can I break its beauty's dainty spell?
> I beg for water from a neighbor's well.

What a difference in tone and feeling between the two translations! The first is more compressed and suggestive, and speaks metaphorically of the well-bucket being "captured" by the flowers. The second, more explicit, concentrates more on the man and his feelings, and uses the metaphor of the flowers casting a spell or charm over the bucket. Yet both translations were done by noted scholars who were doing their absolute damnedest to capture the spirit of the original. No wonder Cervantes had Don Quixote remark, "Translations are the opposite side of the tapestry"—faded reflections of the original language.

Translation is a tough job, rather like having to describe a beautiful piece of sculpture to a blind person. You can tell him what the figure is about, but you can never explain the line and the color, nor the way the light plays across the sculptured stone. You can communicate the content, but not the form. And in art, form is all the difference.

The greatest poems in the world continue to defy translation into another tongue. Goethe's "Wanderers Nachtlied" is considered by many to be *the* most beautiful German poem. Dozens of translations exist, and most people think that not one of them comes close to the musical beauty of the original. But judge for yourself. Here is the poem in the original German:

> Über allen Gipfeln
> Ist Ruh,
> In Allen Wipfeln
> Spürest du

Kaum einen Hauch;
Die Vögelein schweigen im Walde.
Warte nur, balde
Ruhest du auch.

Even if you don't know German, you can feel the simplicity
of the poem. There are only twenty-four words in all, and if
you speak the words out loud, you discover that the *sounds* of
the poem are as important as its meaning, the soft, soothing
s's and *w*'s that sound like trees whispering in the wind. In
fact, that's partly what the poem is about—trees. Now, see
what happens to the poem when it is translated into English—
in this case, by Henry Wadsworth Longfellow:

O'er all the hill-tops
Is quiet now,
In all the tree-tops
Hearest thou
Hardly a breath;
The birds are asleep in the trees;
Wait; soon like these
Thou too shalt rest.

As you can see, the soft sounds of the original—such an important part of the poem's effect—have been lost, and instead, Longfellow has had to substitute the relatively harsh
poetic "thou" and "shalt." Even the meaning has been altered—as you can tell when you compare Longfellow's translation with this one by George Sylvester Viereck:

Over the tops of the trees
Night reigns. No breath, no breeze.
Never a voice is heard
Of rustling leaf or bird
    The forest through.
Hush! But a little ways
From where your footstep strays
    Peace awaits you.

It reads like a completely different poem from the Longfellow translation, doesn't it? Which translation is the most accurate reflection of the original poem? Well, that depends on what you're looking for. Viereck's tries to preserve the soft sounds and the rhyme scheme, so it's closer to the feeling of the original poem. On the other hand, in order to get the lines to rhyme in English, Viereck had to take more liberties with the meaning, so Longfellow's translation is closer to what Goethe actually said. Both versions lack something, and neither has anything close to the beauty and power of the original.

The same problem arises when you try to translate works of English literature into another language. People who don't speak English will never know the true majestic beauty of Shakespeare's poetry. Rudolf Flesch took a famous passage from *Macbeth*—you know the one:

> Out, out, brief candle!
> Life's but a walking shadow, a poor player
> That struts and frets his hour upon the stage,
> And then is heard no more; it is a tale
> Told by an idiot, full of sound and fury,
> Signifying nothing.

He compared this with eight different translations in his native German. The results were depressing. "Struts and frets" was translated eight different ways, including "makes a noise and raves," "swaggers and gnashes," "labors and raves," "stilts and gnashes," "parades and raves," "rages and storms," "stilts and brags," and just "boasts." The word "idiot" translated five different ways, as "blockhead," "fool," "madman," "simpleton," and "ninny." And finally, the immortal phrase "sound and fury" came out in German, variously, as "noise and rage," "flood of words," "storm and urge," "tone and fire," and "pomposity." Think of a German reading something like this:

> Out, out, short candle!
> Life's but a walking shadow, a poor player
> That swaggers and gnashes his hour upon
>   the stage
> And then is heard no more: It is a tale
> Told by a blockhead, full of a flood of words,
> Signifying nothing.

—and believing he is reading Shakespeare. The idea of that passage may have survived the translation, but precious little else did.

Actually, even English speakers don't really experience the language of Shakespeare as he meant it to be. As Sam Johnson pointed out, time has so changed the meaning of the language since Shakespeare's day—even the way the words are pronounced—that the total effect of Shakespeare's poetry today is far different from what it was in 1600 when it was written. It is simply not possible for a twentieth-century audience to hear or experience the plays as Shakespeare's contemporaries did.

Sometimes the imperfect nature of translations has far-reaching effects. The King James Version of the Bible is, of course, a Christian translation from the original Hebrew. A critical Old Testament passage (Isaiah 7:14) is read in the King James version as:

> Therefore the Lord shall give you a sign;
> Behold a virgin shall conceive and bear
> a son, and shall call his name Immanuel.

This became the cornerstone of the New Testament Christian theology, the first expression of the idea of the Virgin Birth. But in the original Hebrew, the passage actually reads:

> Therefore the Lord shall give you a sign;
> Behold a *young woman* shall conceive and bear
> a son, and shall call his name Immanuel.

A small difference, but a crucial one. The word "virgin" had been introduced in the King James translation by Christian scholars trying to prove that the Old Testament prophesied the New. Generations of Jews who would not accept the doctrine of the Virgin Birth were persecuted because of an imperfect translation of their own language! There can be no more apt or bitter illustration of the power of words to shape our reality.

The King James translation of the Bible, so-called because it was commissioned by King James I of England, "cleans up" Biblical passages that were a little too risqué as they read in the original Hebrew. For example, in Deuteronomy, the King James Version says of Moses:

> And Moses was an hundred and twenty years old
> when he died: his eye was not dim nor his natural force
> abated.

A harmless passage, which seems to say merely that Moses was still a strong man when he died. In the original Hebrew, this same passage reads:

> And Moses was an hundred and twenty years old
> when he died: his eye was not dim and his moisture
> was not fled.

There is less pussyfooting in this version; clearly, Moses is still sexually active at 120 years of age—an encouraging thought for Jews and Gentiles alike.

While the King James translation may be guilty of an occasional whitewash, it is unquestionably the source of some of the most beautiful poetry in the English language. Recently, there have been some new translations of the Bible—one a Catholic version, one a closer reflection of the Hebrew original, and one a new "International" edition. This last translation tried to bring the language of the Bible closer to the language of everyday speech—an admirable goal, except that the results are too often laughable. Witness this rendering of the famous "Vanity of vanities, saith the Preacher" passage:

> A vapor of vapors! Thinnest of vapors!
> All is vapor!

The tone of hysteria in that passage reminds one of a familiar horror movie scene: A woman stands in a corner screaming as a green gas comes trickling out of the air vent. If you continue along those lines, you may wind up with a Genesis that looks like this:

> And God said, "Gee, can we have a little
> light around here?"

Granted that translation is a much greater problem than most people realize, there's still the question, "Why are so many words 'untranslatable' into another language?" Partly because we don't learn words by looking them up in the dictionary. We learn them by hearing them used in a context. From the time we are little, we hear a given word used in thousands of different contexts, and each context adds a little something new to our understanding of the meaning of the word.

For example, when you were a child, you probably heard your parents talk about the "nice" day outside, and when you went for a walk with your mother, you noticed it was sunny and warm and she took you to the park to play. Then you heard them refer to the cuddly, four-legged creature who lived next door and played with you as a "nice" doggie. So you thought you had the definition of "nice" all set. But then one day, you got the measles. You felt very sick and late in the day your mother brought you some funny-colored stuff on a spoon that she called the "nice medicine that will make you all better." Since your mother told you it was "nice" medicine, you decided to try it. You took one gulp and discovered that it tasted awful—awful enough that you choked and gagged and made a terrible face. *Nice* medicine, your eye! Already your definition of "nice" is acquiring certain complexities that can't be found in a dictionary definition. It keeps getting more and more complex, too—as you learn that a clean shirt is "nice" and a dirty shirt isn't, that the quiet, skinny, unpopular girl down the street is "nice," while the good-looking one with all the boyfriends isn't, that kissing your baby sister is "nice" but hitting her definitely is not.

What this adds up to is that words have emotional colorations or associations that go beyond the strict dictionary definition. These emotional colorations are called connotations, and connotations are what evaporate in translations. Why is it so impossible to translate connotations? Because you only learn the connotations of a word by hearing it in a wide variety of contexts. Usually, the only people who do this are those who speak a language natively—or at least fluently. Those who learn a language out of high-school grammars and Berlitz phrase books are not aware of the important differences that connotations can sometimes make. Take the example of the Russian prince in love with a beautiful English lady. A romantic man, he tried to tell his ladylove that when he looked at her, time stood still. Unfortunately, this thought emerged in his imperfect English as, "You have a face that stops the clock." The lady slapped his face.

The more contexts a word is used in, the richer its connotations. Compare, for example, the words "home" and "house." Which would be harder to translate? "Home," of course, because it is much more connotatively rich. A foreigner can readily grasp the concept of "house" as the place where one lives, the roof and four walls that provide one with shelter. But "home"—that place "where the heart is"? That place which we treasure "be it ever so humble"? That place which the chariot is "comin' to carry us to"? Cowboys find it out "on the range" (so do the deer and the antelope, who like to play there); baseball players find it near the catcher's position. A home can be broken without the structure of the building being damaged in any way. It would be very difficult for anyone but a fluent speaker of English to understand all the complex associations we have with a simple word like "home."

To see how quickly words acquire connotations that are difficult to explain and almost impossible to translate, look at these next few sentences, which give several different contexts for the nonsense word, "mumsy."

—Tired of having to fight that mumsy feeling
all day? Take Geritol and you'll feel more alive.

—The mumsy lines around her lovely mouth only
added to her beauty.

—I'm not tired or sad, just mumsy.

—They kissed and walked together, hand in hand,
under the peaceful, mumsy evening sky.

—The mumsy notes of the nightingale's song
pierced the still night air.

Having seen the word in just five simple contexts, it would already be hard to give a simple, one-word definition (try it, if you doubt me). Instead, you are left with a lot of vague, hard-to-define *feelings* about the word "mumsy." Those are its connotations.

Why does it matter that words have emotional colorations? Because our ideas and behavior are affected by them, that's why. Those who understand the power of language can do a lot with the skillful manipulation of words. The following passage, for example, describes a secretary named Nina:

Nina, in the anteroom, was seated at her typewriter. Her slender fingers played lightly over the keys. Her blonde hair fell softly to her shoulders. Occasionally, she paused to gently flick one stray lock off her forehead. Her white skin shone with a translucent delicacy.

There was a knock on the door and a man entered. Nina looked up at him and smiled. She had a way of making every male feel that he was the one man in the world she wanted to see. "May I help you?" she said in a well-cultivated voice.

Obviously, that description of Nina is loaded with words that have very positive connotations. Now see how differently the same girl engaged in the same activities can appear when I substitute words with negative connotations:

Nina, in the anteroom, was sitting at her typewriter. Her skinny fingers moved across the keys. Her bleached hair hung limply to her shoulders. Occasionally, she stopped to push one messy strand back from her forehead. Her pasty skin was shiny and one could see the blue veins underneath the surface.

There was a knock on the door and a man entered. Nina stared at him and grimaced. She had a way of making every male feel he was the last man on earth she wanted to see. "May I help you?" she said in an affected voice.

When you compare these two descriptions, you see how emotionally colored words have influenced your feelings about Nina. If you didn't have the two versions to compare, you might think you were judging Nina on the basis of the "facts."

You can have all kinds of fun coloring with words once you get the hang of it. Bertrand Russell is credited with this famous grouping of same-meaning-but-differently-colored words:

> I am firm
> You are obstinate
> He is a pig-headed fool

A popular magazine had a contest in which they invited its readers to send in their own examples. Some of the best of them:

> I am fastidious
> You are fussy
> He is an old woman

> I am sparkling
> You are usually talkative
> He is drunk

> I am beautiful
> You have quite good features
> She isn't bad-looking, if you like that type.

> I day dream
> You are an escapist
> He ought to see a psychiatrist

> I have about me the subtle, haunting fragrance
>   of the Orient
> You rather overdo it, dear
> She stinks.

As semanticist and Senator S. I. Hayakawa has remarked, "Finest Quality Filet Mignon" is just another way of saying "First Class Piece of Dead Cow." The thing itself doesn't change, but our perception of it does—shaped and formed anew by language.

Sometimes the emotional coloration of words affects us in more serious—and insidious—ways. For example, in my classes I do a little experiment. I ask my students to jot down, as quickly and spontaneously as possible, a list of associations with the word "black." Just anything at all that occurs to them when they think of "black" or "blackness." Then I ask them to make another list of associations, this time for the word "white."

Afterward, we compare the two lists. The results are interesting. Most people have very negative associations with the word "black," so their lists have words like "evil," "witch," "bad guy," "death," "dirt," "fear." Nothing good ever seems to come with the word "black" attached. We "blackmail" someone when we force him to pay us money he doesn't want to; we "blackball" someone we don't want to be included; we "blacklist" people and get them fired from their jobs. If you don't like someone you have "black thoughts" about him, and a thoroughly evil man is a "black-hearted devil." You don't have to know what happened on a "Black Monday" to agree that it's not anything to commemorate joyously. Martin Luther King pointed out the negative connotations of the word "black," and Ossie Davis, the black actor, poet, and playwright, reported that Roget's *Thesaurus* lists "120 synonyms, 60 of which are distinctly unfavorable, and none of them even mildly positive. Among the offending 60 were such words as: blot, blotch, smut, smudge, sully, begrime, soot, becloud, obscure, dingy, murky, low-toned, threatening, frowning, foreboding, forbidden, sinister, baneful, dismal, thundery, evil, wicked, malignant, unclean, dirty, unwashed, foul, etc. . . . not to mention 20 synonyms directly related to race, such as, Negro, Negress, nigger, darky, blackamoor, etc."

What about the list of associations with the word "white"? Just what you'd expect—most connotations of "white" are very favorable, and include "purity," "cleanliness," "snow," "happiness," "innocent," "honorable," "weddings," "white knight," "good guys," etc.

What does this all add up to? Clearly, the emotional colorations of two words, black and white, help to shape our attitudes toward black and white *people.* Ossie Davis goes so far as to claim that "Any teacher, good or bad, white or black, Jew or Gentile, who uses the English language as a medium of communication is forced, willy-nilly, to teach the Negro child 60 ways to despise himself, and the white child 60 ways to aid and abet him in the crime." You may think the statement extreme, but a little boy who learns that it is nasty to come to the table with "black" hands, and that people at a funeral wear "mourner's black" and then is told that *he* is also "black," is in the process of transferring negative feelings from the concept to himself.

We're so used to referring to people as "black" and "white" that it's difficult to realize that no one is *really* colored black or white—no one is the color of tar or a bed sheet (and if he is someone had better be around to administer last rites). Most "black" people would be more aptly described as "tan" or "brown" or "chocolate," and whites should really be called "beiges" or "pinks" or "khakis." Certainly "Caucasian" won't do—that sounds more like a kind of shoe than a human being. ("May I see the Caucasians in a size 7B, please?")

At some point in history, a white man first gazed upon the Negro race, found them strange and probably fearsome, and labeled them "Black"—an emotionally loaded word that may have been a reflection of his own hostility and fear. The point is not that language *created* the white man's fear and dislike of the black race—the roots of our racial problems are social and cultural, not linguistic. But our prejudice is a virus in the bloodstream of our language that is passed down from generation to generation.

Of course, "black" is by no means the most negatively charged word we use to describe a person's race. For fighting words, our English equivalent of "*Schweinhund*" could well be "nigger" (the insulting derivative of "Negro" from the Latin "niger," meaning black). Words like "nigger" are highly charged because they are so seldom used. We store them away in hidden closets of bigotry and only drag them out in moments of great passion or hatred.

There's a sequence in the film *Lenny*, about the comedian Lenny Bruce, that makes this point nicely. Lenny (played by Dustin Hoffman) is doing a nightclub act. Suddenly, in the middle of the act, he stops and asks the stage manager to turn on the houselights so he can see the audience. When the houselights are on, he asks, "Are there any niggers here tonight? Any niggers?'' The word runs through the audience like electricity. Everyone immediately stops laughing—the man's just said the unspeakable. Does he know what he's doing? There is much shifting of seats and everyone averts his gaze. Lenny keeps pushing it, though, finally going over to one black man and saying, ''Well, here's *one* nigger. Do I see two? Ah, yes, there's two more niggers over there.'' Then, up close to one angry-looking black man, ''And here's another. Here's one thick, hunky, bunky *boogy!*'' The man looks as though he's going to punch Lenny in the face, but Lenny moves on. ''There's two more niggers over there. And between those two niggers sits a kike. And there's another nigger. That's two kikes and three niggers.'' When the audience finally catches on, the tension eases and soon they begin laughing, as Lenny keeps spinning out his auctioneer's spiel of racial epithets. ''I got three kikes, do I hear five kikes? Five kikes, do I hear six spics? I got six spics, do I hear seven niggers? I got seven niggers. Sold American.'' Just in case anyone listening has missed the point, Lenny adds, ''If the President would just go on television and say, 'I'd like to introduce you to all the niggers in my Cabinet.' And if he'd say, 'nigger-niggernigger niggerniggernigger' to every nigger he saw, until 'nigger' didn't *mean* anything anymore, then you'd never be able to make some six-year-old black kid cry because somebody called him a 'nigger' at school.''

Black people aren't the only ones adversely affected by the emotional colorations of words. Roget's lists the following, among others, as synonyms for ''old'': aged, elderly, wintry, antiquated, archaic, fossilized, senile, decrepit, infirm, aging, senescent, old-womanish, withered, timeworn, hackneyed. Doesn't exactly make anyone pine for his sixty-fifth birthday, does it? This is the way we talk about old people—unless, of course, we are trying to sell them something. Then the tune changes and they become ''seasoned,'' ''mature,'' ''senior citizens.'' (One woman, not about to be taken in, recently

fumed, "Don't call *me* a senior citizen! Just call me a little old
lady.")

English-speaking people internalize these derogatory connotations of the word "old" at a very early age. It is therefore
not surprising that when an automobile driver over sixty-five
years of age annoys a fellow motorist by going too slow, he's
likely to hear:

"Hey, Grandpa, get outta the way! Geez, they should get
these old geezers off the roads, and back into their rocking
chairs, y'know?"

Or: "Watch out, you crazy old gaffer! Why don'cha stay in
the old people's home? Aaaah, go soak your dentures!!!"

This is not to imply that our language is the root cause of
our attitudes toward old people, but words like graybeard,
gaffer, geezer, codger, dotard, old-timer, antediluvian, pre-
adamite, don't help anyone to think kindly about the elderly.
A spokesman for the Gray Panthers, a group that lobbies for
senior citizens' rights, says, "These negative words perpetuate the problem by transmitting negative attitudes towards
old people to new generations of American citizens."

Sticks and stones can only break your bones; words can
really hurt you. Even so innocuous a group as the left-handed
claim to be affected by negatively charged words. This may be
true. Our seven-month baby daughter was showing signs of
being left-handed, and I was not at all happy about it. When
my husband asked me why, I justified the feeling by saying
that most things, from desks and kitchen sinks to eating uten-
sils, are designed for right-handed people. Secretly, I suspect
that my feeling went deeper than that. It's possible, I think,
that I didn't want little Emily to be left-handed because my
language has taught me in lots of small ways that "left" is not
a particularly good thing. After all, who would want to be
"left"—left in the cold, left out, left alone, when you could
be "right"—right-thinking, right-minded, right on! Who ever
heard anyone mourn the loss of his left-hand man? Wouldn't

you rather be adroit (from the French *"droit,"* meaning right) than be *gauche* (French for left)? Or be dexterous (from the Latin for right) than be sinister (Latin for left)? A guy has to be careful about giving a girl a "left-handed" compliment because she might get angry and comment on his "two left feet" and then he would be stuck "way out in left field."

Left-handed people have it easy compared to women when considering the ways our language discriminates. There's an old riddle that goes something like this:

> A man and his young son are in an automobile accident. The father is killed outright and the son is critically injured. The boy is rushed to a hospital for emergency surgery. He is hurriedly prepared for the operation and wheeled to the operating room where the surgeon on duty takes one look at him and says, "My God, I can't operate on this boy; he's my son!"

The riddle is: What was the relationship of the surgeon to the injured boy? By now, this riddle is timeworn enough so that you probably know the answer. You also probably know that when most people first heard it, they couldn't figure out the answer because the idea that the surgeon could have been the boy's mother just never entered their minds. Why? Obviously not because they hadn't heard of a woman being a surgeon, No, it's because the *word* "surgeon" is so strongly emotionally colored. Our language tells us, in effect, "Here is a surgeon. Color him male." Do you doubt it? Then whom do you picture when you think of a "surgeon"? Be honest. Or try this simple fill-in-the-blank quiz that I give my students:

> The doctor is making ———— rounds.
>
> The nurse is making ———— rounds.

If you are like most people, you automatically supplied the word "his" in the first sentence, and "her" in the second.

Thousands of women are surgeons, but in order to be seen in
the mind's eye, they have to be called "women surgeons."
Isn't it odd that we feel the need to qualify only surgeons who
happen to be women in this way? We don't distinguish "tall"
surgeons, or "fat" surgeons, or "nearsighted" surgeons. A
surgeon is a surgeon, whether tall, fat, nearsighted, Jewish,
Gentile—or female.

Our language is loaded with words whose emotional colorations make women seem inferior to men. The pioneer woman
endured all kinds of hardships—bearing and rearing children,
cooking all the meals, baking bread, making soap and candles
and clothes, keeping the house, helping in the fields, shoulder-
ing responsibilities fully as demanding as her husband's. Yet
she is usually described as the pioneer's "helpmate." Would
anyone ever consider describing the man as *her* helpmate?
Not on your history books! History agrees with Blackstone,
who wrote, "Husband and wife are one, and that one is the
husband."

Even simple words like "masculine" and "feminine" are
strongly suggestive of female inferiority. In most dictionaries,
"feminine" is defined as having such qualities as "weakness," "gentleness," "delicacy," "timidity," "passive-
ness," or "submissiveness." "Masculine" is defined variously as having the qualities of "strength," "bravery," "vigor,"
"fortitude," "resolution," "honesty," and "directness." If a
woman reasons clearly and well, she is likely to be told she
"thinks like a man." Witness this exchange between Dean
Martin and Ursula Andress in the movie *Four for Texas*:

Dean: "You aren't thinking about marriage, are you?"
Ursula: "Why should I think about marriage?"
Dean: "That's why I like you, Max. You've got
brains; you think like a man."

A "man-sized" job is a job worth doing, but "women's
work" is petty and demeaning, beneath the dignity of "a real

man." Men who show fear are said to be "womanish," while women who are assertive, dynamic, or ambitious are often described as "mannish," which the *Random House Dictionary of the English Language* defines as "the *aberrant* possession of masculine characteristics" (italics mine). Considering the highly positive connotations of the word masculine, that definition would seem to suggest that if a woman shows the qualities of strength, bravery, vigor, fortitude, honesty, and directness, she is "aberrant."

The emotional colorations of words like "masculine," "feminine," "manly," and "womanish" are internalized at an early age. One recent study of a spelling text used in California elementary schools showed how the bias in our language is passed on to new generations of Americans. In the texts, consonants were represented as little boys, while vowels were little girls. This, supposedly "makes sense" because, as we all know, consonants are "strong," and vowels are "weak." This idea is emphasized again and again throughout the text. The little-girl vowels are all sick, weepy, whining creatures: "Little Miss A," for example, goes "A'choo, A'choo" all the time; "Little Miss I" itches constantly: "Little Miss E" is so weak that she must exercise endlessly; and "Little Miss O" has a sore throat and has to go see the doctor. "Little Miss Y" has no specific health problem, but she is so timid and delicate that she hides behind her umbrella whenever she's outside, saying, "I'm terribly afraid, you see, the sun is really after me!" The boy consonants, in contrast, are active, healthy, fearless—and thoroughly disgusted with the weakling girls. Alleen Nilsen, who conducted the study of the texts, gives a sampling of the different kinds of lines spoken by the boys and the girls:

Boy consonants:
It looks like we are stuck again.
We much prefer to work with men.
You don't look like very much;
You'd probably break at the slightest touch.

Girl vowels:
   Boys, Boys, why must you make fun of me?
   Is it only because I am a she?
Boy consonants:
   Girls, Girls, why don't you smile?
   Can't you be happy for just a while?
Girl vowels:
   Now, now, Mr. Q, depend on me.
   In all your words I'll always be.
   When I'm with Q, I make no sound.
Boy consonants:
   The girls are really getting out of hand.
   I think I'll hit them with a rubber band.
Girl vowels:
   Boo hoo, boo hoo, boo hoo, boo hoo.
   We don't like what you want us to do.
   One sound is hard, as well you knew
   How will we ever remember two?
Boy consonants:
   Vowels, I see tears on every face.
   Enough of this! You'll flood the place!
   Miss O, no complaining, don't you dare!
   Here I come. Beware! Beware!
Girl vowels:
   Oh, please Mr. R, don't change me
   I don't learn too easily!
Boy consonants:
   Little Miss A, now that I stand next to you
   Tell me what you'll have to do.
Girl vowels:
   And when our sounds are short and weak,
   You must make it safe for us to speak.
   Protection is what our short sounds need.
   The boys should protect us—is that agreed?[4]

Is it any wonder that children who are reared on school
textbooks such as these come to have positive associations

with words like "masculine" and negative associations with "feminine"? A follow-up study of the children who had used these texts showed that this was the case: The children identified certain traits such as being sick, being stupid, and crying, as "female," while building things and figuring out solutions were identified as "male."

Women are not always abused by language; sometimes they are simply ignored. Muriel Rukeyser shows how in her "Oedipus Myth Revisited":

> Long afterwards, Oedipus, old and blinded, walked the roads. He smelled a familiar smell. It was the Sphinx. Oedipus said, "I want to ask one question. Why didn't I recognize my mother?" "You gave the wrong answer," said the Sphinx. "But that was what made everything possible," said Oedipus. "No," she said. "When I asked, 'What walks on four legs in the morning, two at noon, and three in the evening?' you answered, 'Man.' You didn't say anything about woman." "When you say Man," said Oedipus, "you include women too. Everyone knows that." She said, "That's what you think."[5]

For years, feminists have been saying that the use of the word "man" to refer to all people renders women invisible—at least in the realm of language. If a woman is killed by a reckless driver, the charge is "manslaughter," if she falls out of a ship at sea, the cry is "man overboard!" There are women who are Congressmen, jurymen, kinsmen, marksmen, statesmen, showmen, tribesmen, middlemen, straight men, and yes-men. One scientific team even went so far as to describe their research as "the study of the development of the uterus in rats, guinea pigs, and men"!

There is no limit to the ways language can be used to make women seem "invisible." When Richard Nixon was choosing his running mate for the 1972 presidential campaign, he didn't want to appear as if he were limiting his search to men, yet he couldn't bring himself to say he would actually consider a "woman," so he remarked, "I will seek as my Vice-President the most highly qualified man or other individual." This statement fits right in with the thinking of one gas station owner in Texas who labeled his rest rooms "Men" and "Other."

Things are getting better, however. With the growth of the women's rights movement, people are becoming more sensitive to the emotionally colored words that reduce women to their sexuality—words like "dolls," "chicks," "dames," "skirts," "broads," and "babes"—and try to avoid them. Still, not too many people ever stop to think of the more subtle ways words are used to indicate that women are first of all women and only secondarily doctors, lawyers, senators, physicists, and even murderers. Feminist writers Casey Miller and Kate Swift have pointed out that headlines like "GRAND-MOTHER WINS NOBEL PRIZE," "BLONDE HIJACKS AIRLINER," "HOUSEWIFE TO RUN FOR CONGRESS," include the kind of description never found in similar articles about men. Can you imagine reading "GRANDFATHER WINS NOBEL PRIZE," "BRU-NETTE MAN HIJACKS AIRLINER," or "HUSBAND TO RUN FOR CONGRESS"? A story about a woman in the news will often comment on her hair, face, figure, clothes. Men are never so favored. Imagine if tomorrow you opened up your local newspaper and read the following article:

Yesterday, State Senator Thomas Friedmann and Lieutenant Governor Richard Terris attended the festive benefit launching the new statewide muscular dystrophy drive.

Blue-eyed Senator Friedmann, the husband of Mrs. Thomas Friedmann, wore a flattering tweed vest set off by a daring green ascot. A former redhead, Senator Friedmann was constantly surrounded by crowds of admirers.

Richard Terris, the pert father of four, also drew admiring glances with his tight-fitting turtleneck sweater, which clung provocatively to his trim, muscular

40-32-36 frame. Dick, who previously served as the Under Secretary of State, was voted "Best-looking Senior" by his high-school class.

The bias of our language affects us even on the very highest levels. There's an old joke from the surgery room that illustrates this nicely. A man is undergoing a major operation when, abruptly, his heart fails. For several minutes, there are no life functions, and he is declared to be dead. But then a famous surgeon rushes in, and using a new experimental procedure, he brings the man back to life. When he returns to consciousness, everyone of course wants to know what he experienced as he lay dead.

"I looked into the very face of God," the man says, awestruck.

"What is He like?" the people ask.

The man answers, "Well, first of all, *She*'s black."

6

Dirty Words

You taught me language; and my profit on't
Is, I know how to curse.

Caliban, *The Tempest*

Today, dirty words are in. No topic is taboo, no parts of the body are "private." The new verbal morality is seen in our TV shows, our conversations, even in our advertising. As adman Jerry Della Femina says:

[The adman] has discovered the vagina and it's like the next thing going. What happened is that the adman ran out of parts of the body. We had headaches for a while but we took care of them. The armpit had its moment of glory and the toes, with their athlete's foot, they had the spotlight, too. We went through wrinkles, we went through diets. Taking skin off, putting skin on. We went through the stomach with acid indigestion and we conquered hemorrhoids. So the adman sat back and said, "What's left?" And some smart guy said, "The vagina." We've now zeroed in on it. And this is just the beginning. Today the vagina, tomorrow the world. I mean, there are going to be all sorts of things for the vagina: vitamins, pep pills, flavored douches like Cupid's Quiver (raspberry, orange, jasmine and champagne).[1]

Men and women alike play the "See-How-Easily-I-Can-Talk-Dirty" game. In nonsexual dialogue, the use of a dirty word is intended simply to impress the listener with one's independence and cool:

> Jane: Wow, that Bloody Mary you made me packs quite a wallop! What did you put in it?
>
> Betty: Simple. The secret's in the Worcestershire sauce. I add a teaspoonful.
>
> Jane: A teaspoonful? Sounds like a lot.
>
> Betty: Wait a minute . . . is that right? Maybe it's a half teaspoon.
>
> Jane: Well, which is it?
>
> Betty: I can't remember now. Oh, what the fuck—start with a half teaspoon and keep adding to taste.

In a sexual dialogue, talking dirty is a strategy of verbal seduction. As Peter Farb, author of *Word Play*, has pointed out, when a man "talks dirty" to a woman, he is preparing by words for a direct physical approach. A woman who agrees to listen to such talk, says Farb, "indicates that she is ready to accept such an approach. Once she has shown her willingness, it is very hard for her to revert to a pose in which she is shocked by the man's physical behavior. She no longer has the option to reject his approach on moral grounds, since she previously signaled her availability by her willingness to listen to the dirty talk." Women also play the verbal seduction game. If a woman uses a dirty word when speaking to a man, she is sending out a signal that she's "experienced" and probably "available." She's broken through the initial barrier of prudery and reserve. Cleverly handled, the use of a dirty word is a veiled and subtle form of seduction.

Another reason people use dirty words is to express contempt for the Establishment, to revolt against people in authority. "Civility is the instrument of the status quo," the say-

ing goes. If you go along with that reasoning, then it follows
that obscenity is the upsetter of the status quo. Dirty words
are a symbol of "honest" rebellion against the verbal miasma
generated by the Establishment.

In the turbulent sixties and early seventies, college kids
across the land used dirty words as a kind of banner to signal
their defiance. Mark Rudd, student leader of the 1968 strike at
Columbia University, explains the rationale behind their use:

> Obscenity . . . helped define our struggle. . . .
> When I told a meeting of the Ad Hoc Faculty Group
> that the talks we were having with them were bull-
> shit . . . the reaction to the style was stronger than
> the reaction to the content. All forms of authority
> [and] traditional "respect" had broken down. . . .

Dirty words became missiles of aggression, a way to provoke
confrontation. Author James Michener, in his account of the
Kent State killings, argues that the students may have been
slain as much for what they said as for what they did. The National Guardsmen who opened fire were incensed to hear obscenities used even by girls who, it appeared to them, could
just as easily have been their sisters back home. In the end,
the Guardsmen felt so "bethumped with words," like Shakespeare's King John, that they fought back with the weapons at
hand—weapons much deadlier than words.

A last, and probably most common, reason why people use
dirty words is to vent their frustrations. Since dirty words are
so emotionally charged, it just *feels* good to let one fly when
you are at the boiling point. As columnist William Buckley
says, there are times when "crap" is just a more satisfying
word than "flapdoodle." Which is why dirty words are used
so often by irritated motorists: "Are you going to cut me off,
you stupid, goddam, son-of-a-bitching asshole?!!!" The car is
really a perfect place for swearing, since it provides a private
forum where you can be as creative with dirty words as you

wish, without worrying about offending anyone who might overhear.

Dirty words are, in fact, a wonderful catharsis that purges the heart and sets the mind to rest. In Rabelais's *Pantagruel*, Panurge says to Friar John, an ingrained swearer:

> "Oh, . . . you sin Friar John . . . it goes against my heart to tell it to you; for I believe this swearing doth your spleen a great deal of good, as it is a great ease to a wood cleaver to cry 'hem' at every blow. . . ."

Used in this way, dirty words are an important form of emotional release. They are only effective, however, when sustained by true feeling. The story is told of an inveterate and colorful swearer whose wife finally rebelled against the constant stream of profanity. To show him what he sounded like, she unleashed at him a string of sustained and eloquent swearing, using his own favorite dirty words. He listened quietly until she had come to the end of her profane litany, and then remarked, "The words are there, my dear, but the music is lacking."

Dirty words do have a kind of special music for which there is no substitute. They are vascular and alive; beside them other exclamations are pale and weak. To quote Buckley again: "It was for the saint that the tushery was invented. 'Tush, tush,' the saint will say to his tormentors as he is eased into the cauldron of boiling oil." In *Anatomy of Swearing*, Ashley Montagu tells of the staff sergeant and the bugler:

> On a certain day the bugler sounded the wrong call. The staff sergeant was about to let loose his figures of speech, when the forbidding eye of the colonel pulled him up quickly. With admirable presence of mind, passion choking him, his face crimson, he strode up to the bugler and, glaring upon the culprit, said, "Oh, you naughty, naughty little trumpeter!"[2]

There's simply no substitute for a dirty word when you're in the mood for one. Few pleasures in life equal that of using a fine dirty word when you've had it up to here (or, more appropriately, down to *there*). English essayist Holbrook Jackson puts it aptly: "Profanity, like Virtue, is its own reward."

But while there is now more freedom to use dirty words than ever before, the self-conscious way we use them only proves that we all still regard these words as "dirty."

What is a "dirty" word? Obviously, it is not "dirty" in itself. A word has no properties of either cleanliness or grime when considered by itself. What's dirty is our feelings about the word and the reality it describes. These feelings are passed on to our children when they first learn that some words are "dirty":

Son: Daddy, what does "screwing" mean?

Father *(cautiously)*: Well, it can mean lots of different things, son.

Son: Is it like when you screw a nail into the wall?

Father *(relieved)*: Yes, son, that's what it means.

Son: Then how come Bobby's brother was talking about screwing a girl from New Jersey. He didn't put her into the wall, did he?

Father: No, son, That's another meaning of the word. When it's used that way it's a very bad word, a dirty word, and not something that nice people go around saying.

Son: Why, Daddy? What does it mean?

Father *(resigned to the inevitable)*: Well, you know how Daddy told you that mommies and daddies sometimes make love to each other? That's what it means.

Son: But I thought you said that when mommies and daddies make love it's beautiful and nice?

Father: That's right.

Son: So why is "screwing" a dirty word? Why, Daddy?

None of us envies the poor father trying to come up with a reasonable answer to *that* one. What answer can there be? Why *is* there a dirty word for lovemaking, if we all think it's beautiful? There are no dirty words for eating or breathing or sleeping. Any sensitive child must suspect that it's not just the *word* that's dirty, but the supposedly "beautiful" act of "lovemaking."

When that sensitive child gets a little older and can understand the metaphorical connection between screwing a nail into the wall and screwing a woman, he can hardly fail to absorb some of the brutal connotations of that "dirty" word. After all, when you screw a nail into the wall, you damage the wood—you destroy part of it. And when you "screw" a woman?

Not all languages have dirty words for sex. Most American Indian tongues don't, nor do Malayan or Polynesian. The Trobrianders find all the words for sex and sex organs perfectly acceptable and proper. But it would be a grievous social error to ask a Trobriander girl out to dinner. She would find your invitation scandalously obscene. That's because their dirty words have to do with chewing and swallowing food. If that seems a little ridiculous to us, the idea of obscenities that are sexual in nature seems pretty laughable to *them*. Which just goes to show that obscenity is in the ear of the beholder.

Indeed, there's really very little rhyme or reason behind the classification of dirty words. Why is a "vagina" (cunt) or a breast (tit) any dirtier than, say, an ear filled with *real* waxy dirt? Why are normal body functions described with "dirty" words—"shitting," "pissing," "farting," "puking"? What is dirty is not the word at all, but our feelings about our bodies and their functions.

The inability to comprehend this simple distinction can lead to absurd behavior. If a child uses a dirty word, a mother may wash his mouth out with soap. This idea that soap (clean) is the proper cleansing agent for speech (dirty) might lead to an interesting televison commercial someday:

> Housewife *(apron on, standing in spotless kitchen)*: Before I got married, I hardly ever used any dirty words. I only had to wash my mouth once every other week or so. But after I married Mac, everything changed. Honestly, the language Mac uses when he comes home from driving that truck!! *(Smiles indulgently at Mac,who has entered from living room reading a Harold Robbins novel).* And then the kids started growing up. *(Another smile at kids, who are fondling each other in the hallway.)* Suddenly, I was washing mouths twice, sometimes three times a day. I just don't know what I would do without my Pure detergent. And Pure gets out that awful ground-in dirt that a big man like Mac gets into his mouth. Right, dear?

> Mac: Right! Shit, that Pure's something special!

> Housewife: See what I mean? Get Pure. It fights the dirt that words put in.

There's a tribe of Australian aborigines who have a custom as quaint as our washing the mouth with soap. If a member of the tribe is overheard swearing by his social superior, he must take a lighted firebrand and pass it close in front of his mouth to "burn" out the dirt. (This may be the reason so few Australian aborigines sport mustaches.) There's also a certain Arab tribe whose members, when cursed, duck their heads or fall flat on the ground so as to avoid a direct hit.

The impact of dirty words comes from the delusion that the *word* has the same power as the *thing*. "Shit" is a dirty word (presumably because saying it is the next thing to doing it), but "shoot" isn't, though its derivation from the former is clear. What special magic in that *i* can change an acceptable remark into one that upsets and appalls so many people? Why are we so disturbed by a simple grouping of four letters? We are confusing our map (language) for the actual territory (the thing itself). Even people who understand the source of this confusion are subject to the power of the "dirty word" taboo. A college professor of linguistics once delivered a tirade to his class on the absurdity and hypocrisy of euphemisms. "The time has come," he said, "for us to drop this false mask of modesty. The study of linguistics has no place for nice-nelly-ism or beating around the bush. To avoid taboo words is to perpetuate their power. The only answer is to adjust to these words, to accept them without embarrassment or shame." At this point, a student asked him to specify which words, exactly, he was talking about. "Why, uh . . ." the distinguished professor stammered, "I'm not sure I can say them in mixed company."

Of course, with time and repetition, some formerly taboo words lose their biting (or fighting) edge. The power of taboo words lies partly in their scarcity of use. Once the words become too-common coin, they are robbed of their power and we have to come up with new and more effective taboo words. "Pain in the ass" and "son of a bitch" used to make people jump a bit, but both epithets are now badly shopworn. In 1936, H. L. Mencken wrote of "son of a bitch":

> There is simply no lift in it, no shock, no sis-boom-bah. The dumbest policeman in Palermo thinks of a dozen better [terms] between breakfast and noon whistle. The term, indeed, is so stale and unprofitable that, when uttered with a wink or a dig in the ribs, it is actually a kind of endearment, and has been applied with every evidence of respect by one United States Senator to another. Put ["you"] in front of it, and scarcely enough bounce is left to shake up an archdeacon. . . .[3]

Many of our saltiest dirty words may soon lose their savor through overuse. Harry Whewell, in an article entitled "The

Crisis in Swearing," frets about the future of swearing and suggests the establishment of a "bad language" commission to help repair the erosion of our dirty word vocabulary. "The time is now ripe," he says, "for such a body . . . to invent and inject into the language a whole series of new swear words. . . ."

> Once devised, getting them into circulation should be easy enough. Television playwrights could be given subsidies for writing them into their scripts. Newspapers could have a "Curse of the Week" corner, and, most useful of all perhaps, the telephone company could introduce a "Dial-a-Swear" service.[4]

But there is one word that time is unlikely ever to wither nor custom stale. Its strength is as the strength of ten. The sound of it is still capable of making some people shudder, and others put up their fists. Edward Sagarin, in his book, *The Anatomy of Dirty Words*, says of this word:

> In the entire language of proscribed words, from slang to profanity, from the mildly unclean to the utterly obscene, including terms relating to concealed parts of the body, to excretion and excrement as well as to sexuality, one word reigns supreme, unchallenged in its preeminence. It sits upon a throne, an absolute monarch, unafraid of any princely offspring still unborn, and by its subjects it is hated, feared, revered, and loved, known by all and recognized by none.[5]

The word is, of course, "fuck."

It is a word known for centuries to every native speaker of English, yet until recently you would have been hard put to find it in a dictionary. It's been banished from all dictionaries since the eighteenth century, when Sam Johnson left it out of his 1755 *Dictionary of the English Language*. Dr. Johnson's discretion was dictated by the times rather than his own preferences, for when a lady seated next to him at a formal dinner party congratulated him on his good taste in omitting "improper words" from his dictionary, he replied, "Ah, so you have been looking for them, madam?" *The Oxford English Dictionary,* the greatest and most comprehensive of all dictionaries of English, which took close to fifty years to compile, totally ignored the word "fuck" until a few years ago, when it finally included it in a *Supplement.* In Wentworth and Flexner's *Dictionary of American Slang,* published in the liberated sixties, it is listed as "fxxk." Try to pronounce that and you may come out sounding like a dandy of the French court:

Louis: Will you walk with me a ways, madame?

Lady: Sire, I am honored.

Louis: It is I who am honored. But stop a minute!

Lady: Sire?

Louis: I have taken too much snuff. Fxxk!!

Even *Webster's Third New International,* a dictionary that has been vigorously denounced for including words like "shit," "cunt," and "prick"—in fact, most of the better-known four- and five-letter words—stops short of including THAT word. In his mammoth work, *The American Language,* H. L. Mencken deals with words like "cock" and "arse" without embarrassment, but does not mention "fuck," referring to it only as "a word of sexual significance."

Its banishment from the dictionary has been matched by banishment from books of all kinds until fairly recently. In 1945, Norman Mailer, no shrinking violet, was reduced to using "fuggin' " in *The Naked and the Dead,* a book which dealt with soldiers who could rarely complete a sentence without using the actual word. Ernest Hemingway, writing in 1940, had his Spaniards uttering absurdities like, "I obscenity into the milk of your mother." Then, in 1959, *Lady Chatterley's Lover* was declared an obscene book and refused passage through the mails by the U.S. Postmaster General. The court fight that ensued resulted in a landmark decision that the use of a word was not in itself obscene as long as it was "not inconsistent with character, situation, or theme." That opened the floodgates. Today the word "fuck" is in common literary and social use. It usually appears as an adjective, used simply for emphasis and without sexual significance: "The fucking door is jammed," "I stubbed my fucking toe," "I've got to have dinner with her fucking parents." Ashley Montagu gives the example of a young man who, when he couldn't get his car to start, said, "The fucking fuck won't fuck," which is about as complete a usage as one could hope to find. Used in this way, "fuck" is a commonplace today. As far back as 1918, it was so common in its adjectival form among British soldiers that, as John Brophy and Eric Partridge have said, "The ear refused to acknowledge it and took in only the noun to which it was attached":

> Thus, if a sergeant said, "Get your ****ing rifles!" it was understood as a matter of routine. But if he said, "Get your rifles!" there was an immediate implication of urgency and dangers.[6]

Overuse had therefore turned the use of "fuck" or "fucking" as emphasis into the exact opposite. If that trend continued, it might have signaled the eventual decline and death of the word. One reason it did not is that in its direct *sexual* meaning, the word is still powerful bad medicine. People who feel perfectly easy about hearing, "It's been a fucking terrible day," will balk if someone remarks that he gave his girlfriend "a hell of a good fucking" the previous night. In his book *Eros Denied*, Wayland Young gives this example of a young man telling of his amorous encounter with a country girl:

> I was walking along on this fucking fine morning, fucking sun fucking shining away, little country fucking lane, and I meets up with this fucking girl. Fucking

lovely she was, so we gets into a fucking conversation and I takes her over a fucking gate into a fucking field and we has sexual intercourse.[7]

In a culture which has long worshiped the ideal of romantic love, "fuck" is too blatantly physical for comfort. Renatus Hartogs, a psychiatrist who has made a study of dirty words, explains our fear of the word: "In a culture where 'love' has meant 'adore but don't touch' . . . 'fuck' is construed as the obverse of love—'touch but don't care.' " The problem really is that "fuck" is just too *honest* a word. It says precisely what it means—and that's a bit too much. We like to think our romances are more spiritual. Think how the substitution of the word "fucking" would destroy our most celebrated love stories. Think of Tristan fucking Isolde. Or Helen of Troy getting a royal fucking from Paris. Imagine Edward VIII of England giving up his throne for "The woman I fuck." It won't do at all; it's just too carnal a description of the act. We would much rather rely on a varied assortment of euphemistic synonyms—"making love," "sleeping together," "lying together," "having sex," or "having intercourse." (The last could as well describe a pleasant conversation at a cocktail party.)

So long as the word is unspoken in polite company, it will remain unspeakable. And so long as it remains unspeakable, it will retain its fine, resounding impact when spoken. It is really our most useful expression of hostility. "FUCK YOU," we scream, and this is supposed to be the ultimate, the worst, the foulest insult of all. Usually, it hits the mark. The hearer is enraged. He is also unable to come up with anything as powerful to say in return, unless he continues to build on the FUCK YOU foundation: "FUCK YOU AND YOUR MOTHER, TOO!!" "FUCK YOU BACK, YOU FUCKHEAD!!!" (Best answer to "FUCK YOU" yet recorded: "Man, you ain't even kissed me yet!!")

The problem is that all this "fuck-youing" becomes rather monotonous after a while. Indeed, when it comes to cursing,

Americans have a limited range. Profanity, as Mencken says, is not an American art. Fuck, damn, shit, son of a bitch—our own cursing is just so damn *predictable*. Samuel Hazo points out that the only thing that made the Nixon Presidential tapes the least bit interesting was the *deletion* of expletives, which allowed the reader to exercise his imagination by filling in the blanks. "Undeleted," Hazo says, "the expletives would have been as boring as barracks-talk."

There was a time when cursing was more imaginative— almost an art form, really. Compare, for example, our mangy lot of curse words with this fine, high-spirited cussin' by French poet Robert Desnos:

> Cursed be the father of the bride of the blacksmith who forged the iron for the axe with which the woods-man hacked down the oak from which the bed was carved in which was conceived the great-grandfather of the man who was driving the carriage in which your mother met your father.

Place that side by side with "FUCK YOU" and you get an idea of the poverty of our own profanity.

Then there's this famous curse, uttered by Bishop Ernul-phus in the eleventh century and directed at certain fancied transgressors of Church law:

> May he or they be cursed, wherever he or they be, whether in their House or in their Fields, or in the Highway, or in the Path, or in the Wood, or in the Wa-ter, or in the Church. May he or they be cursed in Liv-ing, in Dying, in Eating, in Drinking, in being Hungry, in being Thirsty, in Fasting, in Sleeping, in Slumber-ing, in Sitting, in Lying, in Working, in Resting, in Pissing, in Shitting, and in Blood-letting. May he or they be cursed in all the Faculties of their Body. May he or they be cursed inwardly and outwardly. May he or they be cursed in the Hair of his or their head. May he or they be cursed in his or their brains. May he or

they be cursed in the Top of his or their head, in their Temples, in their Forehead, in their Ears, in their Eyebrows, in their Cheeks, in their Jawbones, in their Nostrils, in their Fore-teeth or Grinders, in their Lips, in their Throat, in their Shoulders, in their Wrists, in their Arms, in their Hands, in their Fingers, in their Breast, in their Heart, and in all the interior parts to the very stomach: In their Reins, in the Groin, in the Thighs, in the Genitals, in the Hips, in the Knees, in the Legs, in the Feet, in the Joints, and in the Nails. May he or they be cursed in all their Joints, from the Top of the Head to the sole of the Foot. May there not be any soundness in him or them. . . .

Actually, that's only about one-fourth of the total curse, which is too long to reproduce here in full. The bishop, it appears, was a stickler for detail.

When Shakespeare wanted one character to insult another, he never restricted his man to a simple "damn you to hell." In Act II of *King Lear*, the loyal Kent tells the villain Oswald he is:

A knave, a rascal, an eater of broken meats; a base, proud, shallow, beggarly, three-suited, hundred-pound, filthy, worsted-stocking knave; a lily-livered, action-taking, whoreson, glass-gazing, super-serviceable, finical rogue; one-trunk-inheriting slave; one that would'st be a bawd, in way of good service, and art nothing but the composition of a knave, beggar, coward, pandar, and the son and heir of a mongrel bitch: one whom I will beat into clamorous whining if thou deniest the least syllable of thy addition.

Now, *that's* swearing. Today's man in the street could only reply, "Fuck you, too, Jack!!"

Even primitive tribes show more creativity in their swearing than we. The Wik Monkan tribe of the Cape York Peninsula share our conviction that obscenity is the most effective form of cursing, but their dirty words have much more compass and variety than ours. If you are cursing a man in Wik Monkan, you can either call him "kuntj tantitti" ("fat penis") or "untitti" ("big scrotum"), or "otjumti" ("plenty urine"). The curses for a woman are even more colorful, and include "po'o patj" ("bald pubis"), "po'o ka onk" ("vagina nose," i.e., enlarged clitoris), "po'o tantitti" ("fatty vagina"), or "po'o konnitti" ("big-eared vagina," i.e., enlarged labia minora).[8] These curses are effective because they are specifically tailored by the Wik Monkan to the person he wants to anger and insult, unlike our all-inclusive, To-Whom-It-May-Concern "Fuck you!"

To wrap it up, dirty words are an inevitable, even a necessary part of American culture. Today's loosening of moral codes has brought dirty words into more common use—which may even signal their eventual decline. But as the old dirty words wither and fade away, new ones will be born to replace them. Already we see variations that are more potent than the roots from which they sprang—"cocksucker," "motherfucker." In our society, still grounded firmly in Puritan ethics, there will always be a morality of words, in which sinners are condemned by the wantonness of their language, while just men are known by what they say, not what they do. As an anonymous wit once wrote:

> Oh perish the use of the four-letter words
> Whose meanings are never obscure.
> The Angles and Saxons, those bawdy old birds
> Were vulgar, obscene, and impure.
> But cherish the use of the weaseling phrase
> That never says quite what you mean.
> You had better be known for your hypocrite
>   ways
> Than vulgar, impure, and obscene.
> Let your morals be loose as an alderman's vest
> If your language is always obscure.
> Today, not the act, but the word is the test
> Of vulgar, obscene, and impure.[9]

7

Soft Words

His words were softer than oil, yet were they drawn swords.

Psalms 55:21

Soft words are what we usually call euphemisms, and they derive from the notion that some things, by any other name, would smell much sweeter. Euphemistically, we never vomit, we "whoops" or "upchuck"; we never spit, we "expectorate"; we never defecate, but "eliminate" or "go to the bathroom" (the apparent hope here is that the listener will be left in some doubt as to what happens after we get there). "Feces" becomes "BM" or "poo-poo"; "buttocks" becomes "bottom" or "derriere"; to "sweat" becomes to "perspire," or simply, to "offend." Soft words are a method of denying normal body functions, like the TV commercial that sells "facial-quality" tissue that is not meant for use on faces. The unspoken lesson soft words teach us is that our bodies are something to be ashamed of.

Children learn this lesson at a very early age, when they are introduced to the soft words invented specially for them. Babies learn to "make doody" or "go caca" or "give presents" in the toilet—or rather, potty—when they are around eighteen months old. When they're a little older, they graduate to "making wee-wee" or perhaps "pee-pee" in the potty, too. At last, the great day comes when they are pronounced to be "potty-trained." At this point, maybe even before, they will be introduced to the interesting mathematical concepts "number one" and "number two." A child taught to refer to his waste products in this way can hardly be blamed if he regards them with a measure of detachment—if not downright suspicion.

Children are not the only ones turned afloat in a pastel sea of soft words. We have an entire vocabulary of soft words for our pets. The use of these words doesn't affect the pets, but it does reinforce our assumption that bodies, whether animal or human, are shameful. During a recent visit to my friend Jane's house, she mentioned that she would like me to meet someone. "O-oh, *Teddy*," she called out and into the room raced Teddy—a 220-pound Saint Bernard who seemed to be afflicted with a hyperactive thyroid. He bounded over to me and landed with his front paws in the middle of my chest, spilling some of my tea on my lap. "Oh, don't mind Teddyboy," my friend said. "He's just *so* enthusiastic about visitors." Since Teddyboy at that point had his face next to mine and I could see rows of large, sharp teeth in front, I certainly hoped that what he was feeling at that moment was enthusiasm. "Come here, Teddy," said my friend, and Teddy thundered over to her. He put his huge bear head in her lap (actually, the entire middle section of her body from her chest to her knees) and whimpered. My friend cooed, "Ooooooooh, whatsa matter with my liddle Teddy bear?" It seemed an absurd way to address the beast. "Would you like to go tinkle?"

Teddy went outside to do his "tinkling," which actually seemed more like a waterline break. To call that "tinkling" was a fair match for the remark by the fellow whose hand was in the fire: "I feel a sensation of excessive and disagreeable warmth," he said. Of course, "tinkling" isn't the worst of the soft words we use for pets. That's because "tinkling" is only a substitute for urinating, which isn't *half* so bad as the *other* thing. We'll say almost anything to avoid calling a stool a stool. "Personal business," is very big right now. "Oops, looks like Fido's taking care of his personal business," we titter, as Fido unabashedly spreads his legs and backs up to the tree. Or, "Watch your foot! Fido's got a job to do!" Thank God that Fido probably doesn't know enough English to resent the fact that even so simple a thing as a crap can't be taken in peace without someone popping up to announce it's *work* he's doing and he'd better be sprightly about it.

If we're coy about our pet's excretory functions, we're positively demure about his sex life. In soft speech, two dogs never copulate; they "mate" or "pair off" or "get married" (if you go along with that last one, you presumably believe that most adult dogs are either adulterers or divorcées). Sex organs are described as a pet's "personals" or his "equipment." One lady describes her miniature poodle's penis as "pee-wee" (which surely qualifies him as the Portnoy of the animal world) and his testicles as "Mutt and Jeff." And, of course, if Mutt and Jeff are ever removed, the animal has not been castrated; he's been "altered." Again, the idea here is to find words that signify the animal is different now from before, but not to describe exactly *in what way* he is different. The best example of the extremes we are willing to go to to avoid bringing an animal's sexuality to mind is the nineteenth-century coinage, "gentleman cow," used by the gentility when discussing a bull, that prime symbol of virility and male potency. Which brings to mind the story of the noblewoman of delicate sensibilities who was touring the farming estate she had recently inherited. During the cattle inspection, she happened to catch sight of a bull copulating with one of the cows. She watched, horror-struck, for a moment, then turned to the foreman escorting her. "Why, sir, that cow is no gentleman," she said. "Wal, ma'am," the foreman answered, "actually that gentleman's no cow!!"

Our embarrassment about sex among the animals is surpassed only by our embarrassment about sex among ourselves. Back in the nineteenth century, of course, Victorian morality meant that you could never refer to sex in polite society at all (you could *do* whatever you wanted, you just couldn't talk about it). Victorian standards were so exacting that you couldn't refer to a lady's legs; you had to call them "limbs." ("Call the doctor, quickly!! Regina has fallen and broken her limb!") It was too suggestive when carving the turkey at Thanksgiving to inquire whether one wished the meat of the breast or the thigh, so the terms "white meat" and "dark meat" were coined. The phrase "to give suck" to a baby was also considered far too graphic, and was replaced by the less explicit "to nurse." Nearly a hundred soft words were created to substitute for the taboo word "menstruating"—among them, "having the curse," "feeling that way," "wearing the rag," "flying the red flag," "the Red Sea's in," "little sister's here," and "entertaining the General."

So delicate were nineteenth-century sensibilities that in 1818, Dr. Thomas Bowdler published his ten-volume *Family Shakespeare,* an expurgated version of the plays, whose purpose was to remove "everything that can raise a blush on the cheek of modesty"—which amounted to about ten percent of what Shakespeare actually wrote. (The good doctor's deed is now immortalized in our word "bowdlerize.") In Act II, Scene V of *Romeo and Juliet,* for example, when the Nurse agrees to help the lovers secretly meet, she says to Juliet:

> . . . I must another way,
> To fetch a ladder, by the which your love
> Must climb a bird's nest soon when it is dark;
> I am the drudge and toil in your delight, . . .

Bowdler, protecting the "cheek of modesty" from the naughty allusion to the female pubis, changed the passage to read:

> . . . I must another way;
> I must go fetch a ladder for your love;
> I am the drudge, and toil in your delight . . .

In the *Family Shakespeare*, Falstaff, the lusty and lecherous friend of Prince Hal whose speeches make up at least one third of *Henry IV, I* and *II*, is reduced to quite a minor character; his whore-companion, Doll Tearsheet, is eliminated entirely.

Bowdler, at least, had the good sense simply to omit those characters and lines he felt were objectionable; later bowdlerizers of Shakespeare were foolhardy enough to attempt to rewrite "offending" passages. For example, Iago's famous soliloquy:

> I hate the Moor
> And it is thought abroad that 'twixt my sheets
> He has done my office.

emerges in an edition by Chambers and Carruthers as:

> I hate the Moor
> And it is thought abroad that "with my wife"
> He has "done me wrong."

—which makes Iago sound rather like a jilted cowboy. In another edition, Macbeth's unkind words to a frightened servant,

> The devil damn thee black, thou cream-faced loon!
> Where gott'st thou that goose look?

is changed to read:

> Now, Friend, what means thy change of countenance?

All "improper" words and expressions were carefully removed from Shakespeare's plays by sedulous censors: "damned" became "undone," "whoremaster" became "misleader," "prick" became "thorn." Even Lady Macbeth's sleepwalking soliloquy was not spared: one version has it down as "Out, out, *crimson* spot."

Inspired by the work of the Shakespeare bowdlerizers, Noah Webster decided to publish an expurgated version of the Bible in 1833. His changes included "breast" for "teat," "in embryo" for "in the belly," "lewdness" for "fornication," "lewd woman" for "whore," and to "go astray" for to "go a-whoring." He got rid of the word "womb" altogether by a series of inventive and circuitous phrases.

Today, of course, we are considerably more relaxed about these matters and terms like "turkey breast" have been reinstated. But we're still uneasy when actually talking about things sexual. Most couples simply do not feel comfortable discussing intercourse or sex organs directly and so develop a private sexual vocabulary of their own, like these examples, from the book *Total Sex*.[1]

Intercourse	Male Sex Organs	Female Sex Organs
nuki-nuki	trouser mouse	jelly box
dinging around	joy	flower
tickle your fancy	gratsel	fratsel
joyride	sunup	rosebud

You'd think that a term like "trouser mouse" would make a woman feel somehow uneasy, but apparently even this is still preferable to the word "penis," or even worse, "cock." Our discomfort with the word "cock" once led a man named Amos Bronson Alcox to change his name to Alcott. Amos later became the father of Louisa May Alcott, the author of beloved children's books. One wonders if *Little Women* would have been listed among the forbidden pornographic books if its author had been named Louisa May *Alcox*.

We are equally uneasy about the female anatomy. Witness a foundation manufacturer's recent reference to a woman's "upper frontal superstructure." But this sort of lumbering evasiveness is nothing compared to the problem of describing male and female anatomy in action. We have a veritable lexicon of soft words to describe the act of sex. We like them because none describes what is really meant. "Sleeping with" someone, for example, suggests that you are getting a lot of sleep—which is usually not the case. "Making love" is so demure that it conjures up pictures of a swain down on one knee declaring his affection for his lady. An "affair" sounds rather like the closing of a business deal. "Love affair" is more explicit but still leaves the act itself reassuringly vague. We even have a soft word for the act of rape. A woman is "assaulted," not raped. This can lead to some interesting absurdities, such as the report, in a Boston newspaper, that a man "knocked a girl down, dragged her down the cellar steps, beat her with an iron pipe, and then assaulted her."

We're no more comfortable with the result of sex than we are with the act itself. "Pregnant" is coming back into currency, but still is not quite acceptable in polite society. Soft words are still required where pregnancy is concerned and their numbers are legion. "In the family way" sounds like an economy vacation package. "In an interesting condition" is certainly truthful if not overly specific. "Being with child" sounds as if the baby is somewhere alongside the expectant mother instead of *in*side of her. There are cutesy phrases like "having a cake in the oven" and "getting a new tax deduction" that enable delicate sensibilities to evade the plain fact of incipient motherhood. The most popular of all is "expecting." "Expecting" is a wonderful soft word because it is so delightfully vague, and doesn't specify what the lady is expecting—company? a present? spring? her new mattress and box spring?

If a woman should decide to have an abortion, soft words take the edge off the act. A young woman arriving at a Planned Parenthood center is never asked if she is there for an abortion; instead, the counselor inquires whether she wished a "termination of pregnancy." The developing fetus is never called a fetus—or worse yet, a "baby"—but an ovum, or even a "growth" (suggesting the fetus is a malignancy that has to be removed for the health of the mother). In this case, while the use of soft words may make a scared young woman feel a little better about what is happening, the dangers of describing an abortion in this way are obvious. The reality of what occurs is thoroughly obscured in words.

Clearly, we are uncomfortable with the idea of the human body. We are even more uncomfortable with the idea of a *dead* human body. Well may one ask today, "Ah, death, where is thy sting?" The unhappy answer is that the sting is concealed within the soft underbelly of our language. Nothing is what it appears to be in a funeral service. There is no corpse here, only a "loved one." Undertakers—er—morticians adore that term, "loved one," and generally try to fit it into every other sentence. It is a restful moment in any funeral parlor when a mortician is not referring to the "loved one." There is no coffin here, only a "slumber bed." Much is made of the quality and endurance of "slumber beds"—one Indianapolis mortician even advertises that his "beds" have a "lifetime guarantee." (A safe enough guarantee when you consider the unlikelihood that the customer will ever bring it back for repair.) Dead people are, of course, no longer buried. They are "interred." Or, as Evelyn Waugh has his mortician explain in *The Loved One,* normal disposal is by "inhumement, entombment, inurnment, or immurement," but many people just lately prefer "insarcophagusment." In Waugh's novel, which is no exaggeration of the facts, the bereaved is met at the door of "Whispering Glades Memorial Park" by a "mortuary hostess" who asks him if he is there to make a "Before Need Reservation" for himself. When he makes it clear that he is there to make arrangements for a "loved one," they begin an extended conversation about the details of the funeral, including the following:

> "And how will the Loved One be attired? We have our own tailoring section. Sometimes after a very long illness there are not suitable clothes available and some-

times the Waiting Ones think it a waste of a good suit. You see we can fit a Loved One out very reasonably as a casket-suit does not have to be designed for hard wear and in cases where only the upper part is exposed for leavetaking, there is no need for more than jacket and vest. . . . What did your Loved One pass on from?"

"He hanged himself."

"Was the face much disfigured?"

"Hideously."

"That is quite usual. Mr. Joyboy will probably take him in hand personally. It is a question of touch, you know, massaging the blood from the congested areas. Mr. Joyboy has very wonderful hands."

"And what do you do?"

". . . I brief the embalmers for expression and pose. Have you brought any photographs of your Loved One? They are the greatest help in re-creating personality. Was he a very cheerful old gentleman?"

"No, rather the reverse."

"Shall I put him down as serene and philosophical, or judicial and determined?"

"I think the former."

"It is the hardest of all expressions to fix, but Mr. Joyboy makes it his specialty—that and the joyful smile for children."[2]

There are those of us who wish to avoid this sort of unseemly posturing when we are dead, and choose to be cremated, and so reduced straight off to a nice, no-nonsense heap of ashes. But while you may appear to the naked eye to be a heap of ashes, you are in fact become the "beloved *cremains*" of yourself, and so will be subjected to "interment" in one of an assortment of "Eternal Peace Vessels." The beloved *cremains* may then be transported to a final "resting place" in a special vault of the cemetery—er—memorial park.

Morticians are not the only professionals to upgrade their image by renaming it. "Real estate" people long ago adopted the more sonorous title of "realtors," and mastered the art of selling the customer with soft words. If a "realtor" tells you that the house he's going to show you is "adorable," it means it's small. If he tells you there's a cheerful "eat-in kitchen," it means there's no dining room. A "starter home" is cheap—and cheaply made. And a "fixer-upper" is usually a house that's been abandoned as unlivable by its previous owners.

These days everyone seems to be getting into the act. A car mechanic is no longer a car mechanic, but instead (often as the result of a one-year course of study at a local trade school), a "Doctor of Engines." Gardeners are "landscape architects," plumbers are "water systems specialists," tree trimmers are "horticultural surgeons." The neighborhood dogcatcher has become the "canine control officer." In Germany, where prostitution recently was legalized, a man so moved can go to one of a number of "eros centers," where upon payment of a reasonable fee, he can be "entertained" by the "erostess" who appeals to him.

Heaven only knows what an "engineer" is anymore, since anyone and everyone seems to be one—garbagemen are "sanitary engineers," rat catchers are "exterminating engineers," janitors are "sanitation engineers," housewives are "domestic engineers." *The Engineering News Record,* the now-defunct trade paper of legitimate engineers, used to devote a column to the latest crop of "engineers" appearing on the American scene—among them, a tractor driver who billed himself as a "caterpillar engineer" and a hairdresser who announced he was an "appearance engineer." One woman who worked for a department store as a salesclerk in the home furnishings department went so far as to style herself an "engineer of good taste." H. L. Mencken cites the example of a bedding manufacturer who "first became a 'mattress-engineer' and then promoted himself to the lofty dignity of 'sleep engineer.'" Mencken adds, "No doubt he would have called himself a 'morphician' if he had thought of it."

Some titles are so inflated they threaten to disconnect from the job entirely, conveying no idea at all of what the person actually does. If you met a man who told you he was in the "reused metal products industry," would you know that he was a junk dealer? If someone said he was a "multimedia systems technician," would you be able to tell he was a film projectionist? What about a man who bills himself as "a refuse transport systems analyst," meaning that he is a sewerman?

It would appear that the dwindling number of people who are not "engineers" are vice-presidents. Give a man a "vice-president" title and you will not only change his concept of his job, but also the attitude of those he deals with. Wouldn't you rather deal with a "vice-president in charge of sales" than a simple "sales manager"? Administrative vice-presidents, marketing vice-presidents, assistant vice-presidents (or vice-vice-presidents) are proliferating faster than rabbits. The day can't be far off when cleaning women will be known as "Vice-Presidents of the Latrine."

Euphemisms for things are almost as common today as for occupations. Prisons are "correctional facilities" or "centers for rehabilitation." Tiny, little small-town colleges are "universities." Used cars are "preowned," and reruns are "encore telecasts." One is no longer "fired"; one is "selected out" or "non-retained," or even, simply, "released." (The president of Marine Midland Banks of New York once referred to the abrupt dismissal of three hundred executives as "recent redundancies in the human resources area.") Even certain personality traits emerge in softspeech strangely transformed, not to say rehabilitated. A spoiled brat is described as a "hyperactive child." An academic failure is an "underachiever," and a person who is promiscuous is a "swinger." Peggy Bainbridge was particularly interested in the softspeech used by schoolteachers to explain children's behavior to their parents. Here are some of the ones she came up with:

What the Parent Hears	What the Teacher Means
George's social adjustment has not been quite what we hoped.	The kids all hate George.
Debby is overly interested in the work of other children.	Debby copies every chance she gets.
Bruce doesn't always respect the property of others in the class.	Bruce steals like crazy.
Jane is exceptionally mature socially.	Jane is the only girl in fifth grade with pierced ears, eye shadow, and dates.

Lots of soft words are useful and don't do any discernible harm. It probably makes a teenager feel better to think that he has "blemishes" rather than "pimples." And Grandpa may be better able to preserve his dignity if he can talk about his "dentures" instead of his "false teeth." Now that TV advertising is promoting products like toilet paper, laxatives, and the like, we are awash in soft words. On TV no one gets constipated or has an attack of diarrhea, they experience "irregularity"; people don't perspire, they get "underarm wetness"; women don't have wrinkles, they have "age lines." These are harmless deceits. They seem to make people feel good about themselves, and they don't really *fool* anybody.

The disparity between soft words and the world they describe gets a little more serious when sealskin manufacturers call the slaughter of seals "harvesting." The word "harvesting" suggests green, growing things, ripe and ready to be picked, and has very little to tell us of the brutal reality of a seal harvest, in which men corner a herd of seals and club to death the males, females, and babies. (The hunters use clubs because they don't want to mar the hides with bullet or spear holes.) The word "harvesting" has proved so popular it's been adopted for other forms of hunting: "Neighboring Vermont deer hunters are reporting 14 percent less deer harvested this year than last. A total of 8,264 were taken this season. . . ." These deer were not merely "harvested"; some were "taken." Another interesting soft word. "Taken where?" one might ask. To the farm? To a zoo? To a wildlife preserve? Or to the Great Salt Lick in the Sky?

The use of soft words in this way is a more dangerous reconstruction of reality than calling vaginal douches "feminine hygiene items" or the vomit bags on airplanes "air sickness containers." The intent here is to mislead people.

In late 1977, the Pentagon tried to slip funding for the neutron bomb through the Senate Appropriations Committee by referring to it as "an enhanced radiation warhead." And it *would* have slipped by unnoticed but for the efforts of an investigative reporter for *The Washington Post,* who discovered the deception and brought it to the Committee's attention.

Even the horror of war can be made to seem aseptic and abstract when described with soft words. We are by now all familiar with the examples: "free fire zone" means shooting at anything that moves, whether man, woman, or child, friend or enemy; "pacification" of a village means that most of the inhabitants are killed or sent away to refugee camps; "resource control program" means all the trees and animals in a given area are burned to the ground; "antipersonnel" weapons means weapons designed chiefly to kill people, although we might be tempted to classify it among antiperspirant sprays. In this case, words are no longer a reflection of the truth, but a substitute for it, a substitute so clever and satisfying that finally it can deceive even the men fighting the war. One U.S. Air Force colonel exasperatedly remarked to reporters: "You always write that it's bombing, bombing, bombing. It's *not* bombing! It's air support!" As semanticist Neil Postman says,

"If you change the names of things, you change how people will regard them, and that is as good as changing the nature of the thing itself."

Given this ability of soft words to change the way people regard things, it was inevitable that they would be used to cover up military blunders and defeats. During the Vietnam War, if the army announced it was carrying out a "strategic retrograde action," it meant that our soldiers were in retreat. On one occasion, an artillery commander reported the "accidental delivery of ordnance equipment." That sounds like a rather innocent mistake, one that could quickly be rerouted to its proper destination. Unfortunately, what this described was, in fact, the mistaken shelling of our own U.S. Army troops. American servicemen have a name for language like this; they call it "CYA"—"cover your ass."

This kind of softspeech penetrates to the very highest levels of government. No less a personage than former Secretary of State Henry Kissinger once said that he thought it not impossible that the United States might become involved in a limited nuclear war. The war, he said, would take the form of "local actions" which would have the effect of shifting the risk of initiating all-out war to the Soviet side. Now a "local action" sounds rather innocuous, until you reflect that the attacks on Hiroshima and Nagasaki, the only places where nuclear weapons have ever been used against people, resulted in suffering and carnage almost beyond human imagining—yet these were strictly local actions. What is most threatening, of course, is how Kissinger's adroit use of soft words helped prepare the audience hearing it to accept the unthinkable.

In fairness, we should observe that there are instances in which soft words can be used for more constructive purposes. In fact, one soft word, aptly used, may have saved us from an all-out nuclear war during the Cuban missile crisis of October 22–28, 1962. The question then was whether we dared to establish a "blockade" of the Cuban coast. A blockade is an act of war. We wanted those missiles out of Cuba, but we didn't want a war. So what did President Kennedy do? He went ahead and blockaded the Cuban coast, but didn't *call* the action a blockade. He called it a "quarantine"—which is less clearly defined as a warlike action. For the American public, the word also had a useful association with the kind of safety measure taken against a dread "disease." Doubtless, the Russians and the Cubans were not taken in by this wordplay, but we stuck to our own definition of what we were doing, and because they didn't want war either, they accepted it. We accomplished our military objective while letting our enemies know we didn't want war. A blockade took place in the real world and on the high seas but not in the realm of language.

8

Easy Words

Be not the first by whom the new are tried,
Nor yet the last to lay the old aside.

Alexander Pope

"Most wonderful of all are words and how they make friends with one another, being oft associated until not even obituary notices do them part," O. Henry once remarked. And indeed it *is* rather remarkable, given the infinite word combinations possible in the English language, that certain word groupings should be as enduring as they are. It's also rather unfortunate. Loyalty and stick-to-itiveness may be admirable qualities in human beings, but they are not so altogether desirable in words.

Nonetheless, easy words have been around for a long time, and there's no sign that they're about to leave us now. The most common form of easy word is the cliché. The word "cliché" comes from the French, who used it to refer to a metal plate cast from a page of type, with which a printer could make copies of a book without having to reset the typeface. Today it has, of course, lost its original meaning, but the smell of mimeograph ink is still strong.

It's hard to see how some of our most cherished clichés ever got to be so popular, since they make so little sense.

Why, for example, do we always say that army troops "beat a hasty retreat"? Wouldn't it be wiser to beat a careful retreat? A well-organized retreat? A prudent retreat? And why the insistence that troops go on "beating" all these tedious retreats, anyway? We can all appreciate a good rhyme ("beat" and "retreat") but there must be other ways to undertake, conduct, execute, perform, prepare, organize, arrange, carry out, a backward movement of troops than to "beat" a "retreat."

While we're at it, why is it that no one ever seems to experience anything other than a "rude awakening"? Surely some awakenings, even if sudden, are perfectly polite. Why are all struggles "uphill"? Can't a struggle be difficult even if it doesn't defy the forces of gravity? Why does the hero always want to fight the villain "fair and square"? What is there about the lowly square that inspires such faith? Can't a trapezoid be trusted? A rectangle relied on? Russell Baker once lost patience with the senselessness of all the clichés connected with time, and filed this bill of complaint against them:

> Why should time not hang light on one's feet, instead of heavy on one's hands? Try one's body, instead of one's soul? Run long, instead of short, and in, instead of out? Jump up and down noisily, instead of standing still? Bus or drive, instead of flying? Why is time money, but never credit? Ripe, but never green? Why does one have the time of one's life, but never of one's day or week? Why does one arrive in the nick of time, but never in the slash? And is not time not just the great healer but the great sickener of all things?[1]

Clichés don't have to make a great deal of sense. Whether they do or not, people keep using them. A person who wouldn't dream of using someone else's toothbrush will feel not a qualm about using someone else's tired expressions.

Some people become so addicted to clichés that it is impossible for them to talk without them. The cliché expert of all time was surely Mr. Arbuthnot, the creation of Frank Sullivan, who occasionally granted "interviews" like this to *The New Yorker:*

> Q. Mr. Arbuthnot, as an expert in the use of the cliché, you are a pretty busy man, aren't you?

> A. Mr. Todd, you never spoke a truer word. Half the time I don't know whether I'm coming or going. Why taking care of my livestock is a man-size job in itself.

> Q. Your livestock?

> A. Yes. At least once a day I have to beard the lion, keep the wolf from the door, let the cat out of the bag, take the bull by the horns, count my chickens before they are hatched, shoe the wild mare, and see that the horse isn't put behind the cart or stolen before I lock the barn door. . . .

> Q. What else do you do, Mr. Arbuthnot?

> A. Well, let me see. I take into account . . . I put in an appearance, I get the upper hand of, I bring the matter up, and I let the matter drop . . . I take to task, I knuckle down, I buck up, I level criticism, I venture to predict, I inject a serious note, I lose caste, I am up to no good, I am down on my luck, I pass the time of day, I go down to posterity, I cast into the discard—that reminds me, do you realize why I am not wearing any pearls?

> Q. Why not?

> A. Swine got 'em. . . .

> Q. On the whole, you seem to have a pretty good time, Mr. Arbuthnot.

> A. Oh, I'm not complaining. I'm as snug as a bug in a rug. I'm clear as crystal—when I'm not dull as dishwater. I'm cool as a cucumber, quick as a flash, fresh as a daisy, pleased as Punch, good as my word, regular as

clockwork, and I suppose at the end of my declining
years, when I'm gathered to my ancestors, I'll be dead
as a doornail. . . . ²

Parents depend heavily on clichés to subdue their children.
"Get down off there, you'll *break your neck!*" Susie's mother
screams as Susie blithely swings from one branch to another.
Comedian George Carlin says that when he was a kid, "breaking your neck" was one of the only injuries there was—along
with "putting someone's eye out." ("Let go of that stick, you
want to put someone's eye out with that?") No one ever
warned him of a fractured ulna or a scraped knee. Similarly, a
child is never warned that she will feel cold or get the sniffles
if she isn't warmly dressed; she's always told she will "catch
pneumonia." If a child loses something, he's likely to hear,
"Well, it just didn't get up and *walk* away, did it?" If he
doesn't eat his broccoli, he's told to "think of all the starving
children in India." (One boy, determined not to be out-
maneuvered, staunchly replied, "OK, let's send it to them.")
Other familiar childhood clichés: "Don't *pick* at that!" "In or
out, in or out?" and "I suppose if Johnny Peterson jumped off
the Empire State Building, *you* would have to jump off the
Empire State Building."

The most dreaded verbal affliction of childhood is the pa-
rental proverb. "Aw, Mom, do I *haveta* get up now?" comes
the plaintive cry. "Now, now, Michael, you know what they
say—the early bird catches the worm!" Fortunately, many
young children have their own built-in defense against proverbs and clichés; they don't really understand them. This
childish lack of discernment can also be seen in children's
prayers. One little girl, for instance, used to begin her prayers
every evening with the sentence, "Hail Mary, full of grapes."
Another little girl once jabbed her baby brother in the side
when she heard him sing, "Sleep in heavenly beans." "Not
beans, stupid," she scolded him, "peas." Children, being

pragmatists, think more on daily bread than on eternal verities.

Perhaps it's just as well children don't understand the words they recite—particularly proverbs, since these are so seldom true. Proverbs provide little guidance to the real world. Frank Sullivan tells the sad story of a girl who took the old saying about "A stitch in time" to heart:

> She tried such a stitch often . . . but never saved nine, or even two. Her fingers were mainly thumbs when it came to needlework and every time she tried to save nine stitches in time, the thimble fell off her finger, she pricked her finger, her mother had to leave off whatever she was doing and give first aid, the rest of the family had to scout around for the thimble, which was a gold heirloom that belonged to her great-grandmother, and which had rolled down a crack in the floor; and the net result was that the schedule of the household was set back anywhere from half an hour to half a day. My friend estimates that for every stitch she tried to save, either she or those near and dear to her lost an average of fifty stitches. Now, that could mount up to quite a lot of embroidery in the course of a year. . . . [3]

Today, most proverbs make so little sense that they work just as well if you mix them all up together:

> An apple a day spoils the child.
>
> Sparing the rod keeps the doctor away.
> Early to bed and early to rise makes Jack a dull boy.
>
> All work and no play makes a man healthy, wealthy, and wise.
>
> A rolling stone is worth two in the bush.
>
> A bird in the hand gathers no moss.

Deliver these sayings with the appropriate solemnity, and they sound just as good as the originals.

The emptiness of meaning that characterizes most proverbs has led, as such verbal inflation often does, to a revaluation by satire. Many of the best jokes of the sixties were twisted proverbs. Some examples:

A criminal named Stein broke out of jail and escaped into the streets of New York City, followed hotly by the police. He tried every dodge he could think of, but the police stayed hot on his trail. Finally, as he was running by the Time building, he saw a little protected niche in the wall and took cover in it. The police ran past him down the block, and Stein made good his escape. That's how A NICHE IN TIME SAVED STEIN.

Clam fishermen have been pestered for years by terns, scruffy water birds who eat clams, and so compete with the fishermen for their valuable catch. One morning, a group of clam fishermen found hundreds of terns already hunting clams on the beach they planned to fish. Furious, the fishermen decided to chase the birds away by throwing rocks. They could only gather a limited number of rocks on the beach, and before they began the assault, the leader cautioned: "Make every throw count, now. LEAVE NO TERN UNSTONED."

Other punch lines, for which you must supply your own preceding narratives (the originals are too long for inclusion here) are:

A watched bettle never coils.

I wouldn't send a knight out on a dog like this.

People who live in glass houses shouldn't stow thrones.

Twisted sayings like these are called spoonerisms, named for

Rev. Dr. William A. Spooner, renowned for his amusing slips of the tongue. The Reverend unwittingly demolished some of our most familiar sayings: "Work is the curse of the drinking classes," he once said, meaning that "Drink is the curse of the working classes." One day, when giving a speech to a group of farmers, he addressed them as "noble tons of soil." He described the knock-out punch one fighter gave another by saying that "he delivered a blushing crow." His most embarrassing slip of the tongue, however, was the time he rose at a dinner party to offer a toast to Queen Victoria, whom he hailed as the "queer old dean" instead of the "dear old queen."

Spoonerisms point up the fact that some phrases in English are so inextricably wedded they are instantly recognizable even when mutilated. Here familiarity breeds something other than contempt; it breeds indifference. Words worn so smooth through overuse lose all impact and cease to communicate. The bite has long since gone from such common metaphors and similes as "the long arm of the law," "the apple of his eye," "a bull in a china shop," "the milk of human kindness," "the bitter taste of defeat." These expressions, once colorful and imaginative, have lost their cutting edge. Today people use them mechanically, with no thought of what they actually suggest. This explains the growing number of "mixed metaphors"—we should retitle them "nixed metaphors"—one finds today. As a business executive recently remarked, "When you see all those other people getting the ax, it makes you gun-shy." Obviously, "getting the ax" and "gun-shy" no longer call up images in his mind of an ax, gun, or any other weapon. Such metaphors are dead, but we stubbornly refuse to give them a merciful burial, and they meander ghostlike through our speech and across the pages of our writing. Evidence of the terminal decay of meaning is everywhere. Read this sentence from one of Ian Fleming's James Bond books, "Bond's knees, the Achilles' heel of all skiers, were beginning to ache." Or listen to Warren Austin, former United

States Ambassador to the United Nations, counsel the Arabs and Israelis to "sit down and settle their differences like good Christians." Christopher Fry, in his play *The Lady's Not for Burning*, underlines the frequent inanity of clichés when he has the Priest exclaim, "It's Greek to me," then add, startled, "But I know Greek!"

Perhaps it's just as well, in a way, that clichéd metaphors are drained of meaning. We use them so loosely that we would be in trouble if we took them to mean what they suggest. Anyone who actually endured what we *say* he does would be a pitiful creature indeed. Suppose, for example, a woman has ended an unhappy love affair. There are many who would whisper that she "got burned" by her ex-lover. Or perhaps, that she really "took a beating" from him. Of course, they would hasten to add sympathetically, he "twisted her arm" to make her stay with him, but in the end, after months of being forced to "sit on pins and needles," it was she who was "left in the cold" with "egg on her face." Her friends tell her that she was too good for him anyway, but then they turn around and put "a knife in her back" by laughing about how poor dumb Susie "got the shaft." It's undeniably her own fault because she "bit off more than she could chew" and that's why she ended up "in the hot seat," "strung out," "stepped on," "tied up in knots," and "hanging by her toes." Amazing, in view of all she'd been through, that she had enough strength left in her poor broken and battered body to marry on the rebound, thereby throwing herself from the "frying pan into the fire," where, we charitably hope, she will at last be reduced to ashes and forever freed from being stoned, burned, cut up, chewed over, or otherwise tormented.

As if metaphorical tortures aren't bad enough, there's also the slew of clichés that link man figuratively with animals. If we took these literally, we'd all have to surrender ourselves to the nearest zoo, as this passage from a Columbia University Press bulletin neatly points out:

Man . . . is chicken-livered, lion-hearted, pigeon-toed. He is treacherous as a snake, sly as a fox, busy as a bee, slippery as an eel, industrious as a beaver, gentle as a lamb. He has . . . the ferocity of the tiger, the manners of a pig, the purpose of a jellyfish. He gets drunk as an owl. He roars like a lion; he coos like a dove. . . . He works like a horse. He is led like a sheep. He can fly like a bird, run like a deer, drink like a fish, swim like a duck. He is nervous as a cat. He gets hungry as a bear and wolfs his food. He has the memory of an elephant. He is as strong as an ox. He parrots everything he hears. . . . He struts like a rooster and is as vain as a peacock. . . . He is as slow as a tortoise. He chatters like a magpie. . . . He is as dumb as an ox, and he has the back of an ox—he's even as big as an ox. He's a worm. . . . He's a rat. . . . He's a louse.

The real problem with clichés is that stale words lead to stale ideas. Frank Binder, dialectician and scholar, says, "There is no bigger peril either to thinking or to education than the popular phrase." Indeed, clichés are invisible, creeping fungi that feed on the human brain to turn it to rot. They do not perform the principal function of words, which is to communicate thought, for they appeal to attitudes and expectations that are already formed. As Professor I. A. Richards says, "They require no new re-ordering or re-thinking of our experience." They are "easy" words because it's easy to fall back on them rather than attempt new ideas or approaches. Perhaps this is why, as Arlan J. Large said in a *Wall Street Journal* article, clichés and hackneyed expressions are "the mortar of congressional speech." He went on to add that

. . . the middle-aged men who make their living with words feel the need, under the pressure of extemporaneous debate, to use combinations of words they've heard before and are comfortable with. . . .

Senator John Pastore . . . is able to reel off dazzling clusters of bromides in his own speeches, as in this:

"I say today, let us not throw out the baby with the bathwater, let us not lose sight of the forest for the trees, let us not trade off the orchard for an apple. . . ."4

Presumably, Pastore felt that the combination of *three* of these stock phrases would give his rhetoric a heroic effect. The baby and bathwater cliché appears to be a special favorite of Congressmen. Listen to a Senator from Alaska: "It seems that many times when we want to change the water, we wind up throwing out the baby." Or to a Representative from South Dakota: "I do not agree with those here or elsewhere that favor throwing out the baby because of dirty water." There is a plethora of babies and bathwater being tossed around the halls of Congress. Arlan J. Large concludes sadly that after the death of Everett Dirksen, elegant oratory vanished from the halls of the Senate—perhaps because senators no longer have the time to put a high polish on their rhetoric. He adds: "Whatever the reason, the result is an addiction to what's been said before, and it accounts for the sound of all those apprehensive babies sloshing around in their bathwater."

Another Congressional favorite is the expression "a long row to hoe," which has been variously rendered as "a long *road* to hoe," "a long row to haul," and "a long load to haul."

Laziness may explain why so many intelligent people fall back on clichés. Some people, however, use clichés because they think they are impressive-sounding. In fact, clichés are often the coin of the half-educated. Someone who doesn't have a command of language is likely to hear a stock phrase for the first time and be impressed with it. Thereafter he will use it as though he had invented it himself. This is particularly true of foreign-language clichés, such as "coup de grâce," "je-ne-sais-quoi," "fait accompli," "in flagrante delicto," "terra firma." One unfortunate soul seeking to impress a newfound acquaintance bungled his chance when he said, on disembarking from a plane, "It sure is nice to be back on good old terra-cotta again!" John Beaudoin and Everett Mattlin, authors of *The Phrase-Droppers Handbook,* have remarked on the common addiction to uncommon foreign phrases:

> . . . sauce your talk with foreign words or phrases and the banal can be beautiful. Corny or not, you will be labeled a Cultivated Person. . . . The true man (or woman) of the world has the gift of tongues. Speak English alone and you may be alone . . . unrelieved English makes you irredeemably small-town, the sort who spends Saturday night with take-out Chinese food and Archie Bunker. . . .

Latin, they add, is particularly good to cultivate because it is

> . . . Dead, but puissant in death. Say what you will, Latin has power. The speaker isn't merely bright and traveled, someone who's picked up a few phrases, he is *learned,* by God. It all has to do with the glory of the ancients and the language in which they immortalized their wisdom. Latin's dominance as the queen of snob language, is, well, irrefragable. . . .[5]

George Orwell once warned that laziness in speech leads to foolishness of thought. It is just plain laziness to rely on someone else's tired word combinations. They may seem to offer a more rapid, more easily assimilated kind of verbal communication, but the key question is: what is truly being communicated? When the Biblical allusion to the blind leading the blind was first written, it was a fresh perception of all men's ignorance and uncertainty, but now the phrase has been emptied of real meaning. The person hearing it is no longer led to reflect on a truth of the human condition. The familiar sounds activate a reflex that accepts without understanding; the whole transaction takes place on a level somewhat lower than cerebral, say, somewhere down around the medulla oblongata. The same is true of many once meaningful phrases, drained of content through overuse. Even great literature cannot wholly escape the curse of overfamiliarity. There is the story of the man who went to see *Hamlet* for the first time and pronounced it to be merely "A bloody tale, full of quotations."

Catchwords

Catchwords are not exactly clichés, but they are still words we hear so often we become deadened to them. Catchwords are "in" talk, the words we use to show that we are "with it," "right on," and "where it's at." Young people, under pressure to be accepted by a peer group, are particularly susceptible to this kind of easy talk. Thus, when teenagers get together to "rap" you're likely to hear about a really "groovy" or "wild" or "far-out" experience—that is if the participants are really "together" and "doing their thing" and not "freaky" or "weird"—because if they are, they're probably "on a downer" or "up against the wall" and then you're in for a "really heavy trip" as they tell you all about their hangups—which is no fun at all, as anybody who understands all this can tell you. Of course, young people are not the only ones who habitually use catch phrases. In her wickedly witty book *The Serial,* Cyra McFadden satirizes the empty, automatic speech of her Marin County, California, neighbors:

> "I'm going to be really up front with you. I don't know where your head is, but I'm going to tell you what space I'm in. Like, wow. It's really outasight!"
>
> "You and I have to get clear, you know? Right up-

front. I mean, you are into this incredibly destructive bag."6

McFadden's been receiving a lot of phone calls from her disgruntled neighbors, including one who called to complain, "Cyra, are you really into hurting people? Do you really get off on it? I mean, it just blows me away."

Catch phrases have been used so much and so loosely that they have become a kind of substitute for thinking—an automatic response devoid of content or meaning: "I mean, let me tell you, like, it was really something else, would you believe" has more stammer than substance. It may be all right for patchwork jeans or even Baskin-Robbins ice cream to be "groovy," but if wedding ceremonies and Kahlil Gibran and UN Ambassador Andrew Young are also "groovy," then the expression is devalued and the word becomes meaningless. "Groovy" no longer communicates anything specific: it is reduced to a kind of inarticulate cry of pleasure or approval: "Groovy, man, really *groovy*."

Recently, playwright David Mamet was asked by an interviewer how he felt about the reviews of his new play that had opened on Broadway. "Marvy," Mamet replied. "That kind of write-up is yummy." And singer Pat Boone wrote in a religious bulletin, "My guess is that there isn't a thoughtful Christian alive who doesn't believe we are living at the end of history. . . . I don't know how that makes you feel, but it gets me pretty excited. Just think about actually seeing, as the apostle Paul wrote it, the Lord himself descending from heaven with a shout! *Wow!*" Gee whillikers, isn't anything awe-inspiring enough to be above description by a catch phrase? One wonders what Pat Boone's revised version of the New Testament would be like:

And Jesus spake unto Lazarus and said, "Arise and live again!" And Lazarus arose and he did live again. And the people saw. And they were wowed.

The catch phrase "you know what I mean" has become an annoying national habit. So has its abbreviated cousin, "you know." There are people who inject "you know" into every pause in their speech. I once clocked a speaker on TV, replying to an editorial by the station, at twenty-four "you knows" in a single minute! One man was recently overheard to remark to a friend, "You know, you never know!" Louis Lyons, former curator of the Nieman Foundation at Harvard, comments despairingly about "you know": "What does it mean? *What do I know?* What is that expression? A nervous tic? A lack of vocabulary?"

Slogans

Christopher Morley once said that the greatest danger to peace is the military band. Actually, slogans are much more dangerous. At least, when the music stops, it's possible for rational thought to return. But slogans, once heard, often take the place of rational thought. A slogan can be used to whip crowds into an emotional frenzy, precluding any possibility of thoughtful debate and consideration. In World War I, "Deutschland über alles" was cheered by great crowds of Germans, while on the other side of the Atlantic, Woodrow Wilson's slogan "Make the world safe for democracy" was urging Americans on. During the Bolshevik era, the cry "Land, bread, and peace" swept millions of people on to bloody revolt.

Man has always felt the need for some ritualistic cry to help establish him as belonging to a group. Throughout history, elaborate ceremonies featuring group chanting or screaming have served to initiate action. Indian war dances and high-school pep rallies evolved to satisfy the same human need. And, of course, some slogans can serve a useful social function, like the ones we use to cheer on our team at a football game. But semanticist Neil Postman warns that the difference between an utterance like "Go, go, go, Lions" and "Burn, baby, burn" is not so great as some people suppose. In both instances, the slogan is used not only to express but to intensify feelings of hostility. Once you surrender to the seductive security of groupthink, it's hard to get out of the habit.

The problem with slogans is that they're verbal shorthand: they reduce very complex questions or problems to a few catchy words. This leads people to look for all-too-easy solutions and pat answers to problems. In 1946, the campaign slogan "Had enough? Vote Republican" was a clever catchall phrase, since it appeared to offer an answer to every form of discontent—with inflation, or the scarcity of goods during wartime, or the peace settlement, or fourteen years of Democratic rule, or—you name it. In 1968 and 1972, "Peace with honor" sounded just great, but it sidestepped the very complicated question of just what *was* honorable. (As it turned out, it also sidestepped the question of just what was peace, but we didn't know that at the time.) When Barry Goldwater was running for President, he told a TV audience that he wouldn't ban the possibility of nuclear war with Russia because it was better to "die on your feet than live on your knees." The people in the studio responded by cheering, applauding, and whistling their approval. They were, of course, applauding their own potential annihilation. It's hard to believe that any person, in that moment, really envisaged the realities of radiation, famine, millions of dead, the end of human civilization, and everything else implied by "Better to die on your feet than live on your knees." Thinking had been stopped—or at least suspended—by the fine sound of the slogan. "Better dead than Red" usually achieves the same effect. Neil Postman feels strongly that slogans are a serious threat to the future of civilization, and he suggests that "as a general rule, whenever you find yourself applauding, cheering, or chanting in public places, you may suspect that your intelligence has been by-passed."

Slogans recognize no contradictions, no subtleties of thought. "Power to the people" is a slogan few of us would oppose, unless we stop to think what people are being referred to. *All* people? White middle-class American people? Gay people? Or only leftist groups? "Make love, not war": What war? Just the Vietnam War? Make love to whom? Our enemies? Our friends? Perfect strangers? The effect of slogans is to narrow the range of human perception. Their limited ability to convey any meaning is revealed by the fact that slogans are so susceptible to a well-phrased answer—another slogan, in effect. "I found it!" scream bumper stickers of born-again Christians all over the country. "The Jews never lost it!" answer the bumper stickers of satisfied Jews. "Women belong in the home," cries Phyllis Schlafly, militant leader of antifeminist forces. "Women belong in the House—and the Senate" retort the banners of NOW marchers in Chicago. Slogans can even be interpreted in two inimical and contradictory ways. For example, the slogan "Remember the Alamo" is one of our oldest and most cherished battle cries. But in all fairness, one should point out that the Mexicans could have marched even more proudly under a "Remember the Alamo" slogan, since it was *their* victory. Slogans are empty vessels that can be filled with any content.

9

Politics: The Art of Bamboozling Words

Political language . . . is designed to make lies sound truthful and murder respectable, and to give an appearance of solidity to pure wind.

George Orwell

Propaganda. How do we feel about it? If an opinion poll were taken tomorrow, nearly everyone would be against it. For one thing it *sounds* so bad. "Oh, that's just propaganda" means, to most people, "That's a pack of lies."

But propaganda doesn't have to be untrue—nor does it have to be the devil's tool. It can be used for good causes as well as for bad—to persuade people to give to charity, for example, or to love their neighbors, or to stop polluting the environment, or to treat the English language with more respect.

The real problem with propaganda is not the end it's used for, but the means it uses to achieve the end. Propaganda works by tricking us, by momentarily distracting the eye while the rabbit pops out from beneath the cloth. This is why propaganda always works best with an uncritical audience, one that will not stop to challenge or question. Most of us are bamboozled, at one time or another, because we simply don't recognize propaganda when we see it.

Here are some of the more common pitfalls for the unwary:
Name-calling is an obvious tactic but still amazingly effec-

187

tive. It's just what you would expect it to be—calling people names. The idea is to arouse our contempt so that we'll dismiss the "bad name" person or idea without examining the merits.

The old saw "Sticks and stones may break my bones but names will never hurt me" has always been nonsense. Names *do* hurt, and badly, as any child who has been called one can tell you. Name-calling can be devastating to a child's psychological development. Peter Farb classifies children's name-calling into four categories, which he lists in order of decreasing offensiveness:

1. Names based on physical peculiarities, such as deformities, use of eyeglasses, racial characteristics, and so forth. A child may be called "Flattop" because he was born with a mis-shapen skull—or, for obvious reasons, "Fat Lips," "Gimpy," "Four Eyes," "Peanuts," "Fatso," "Kinky" and so forth.

2. Names based on a pun or parody of a child's own name. Children with last names like Fitts, McClure, Duckworth, and Farb usually find them converted to "Shits," "Manure," "Fuckworth," and "Fart." [And little girls with last names like "Woolfolk" usually find it converted to "Willfuck."]

3. Names based on social relationships. Examples are "baby" used for a sibling rival or "chicken shit" for someone whose courage is questioned. . . .

4. Names based on mental traits—such as "Clunkhead," "Dummy," "Jerk," and "Smartass."[1]

Bad names may wreak havoc with a child's ego, but they're even more dangerous when they're used against political opponents, policies, or beliefs. During the vice-presidential debates, when Senator Robert Dole denounced Senator Walter Mondale as "probably the most liberal Senator in the entire U.S. Senate," he wanted conservatives to react blindly, emotionally to the "liberal" label without stopping to consider

Mondale's ideas. Name-calling is at work whenever a candidate for office is described as a "foolish idealist" or a "two-faced liar" or an incumbent's policies are denounced as "reckless," "reactionary," or just plain "stupid." Some of the most effective names a public figure may be called don't really mean anything at all: "Congresswoman Jane Doe is a *bleeding heart"* or "The Senator is a *tool of the military-industrial complex!"*

A variation of name-calling is *argumentum ad hominem,* which tries to discredit a particular issue or idea by attacking a person who supports it. For example, one of Phyllis Schlafly's supporters recently said that she was against the Equal Rights Amendment because "the women who support it are either fanatics or lesbians or frustrated old maids." Aside from the fact that the statistical probability of this being true is nil, it is also specious reasoning. The Equal Rights Amendment should be judged on its merits, not the alleged "personal problems" of its supporters. The fact that Alexander Hamilton was a bastard foreigner born to unmarried parents outside the continental limits of the United States does not reflect on the American Revolution nor on his policies as Secretary of the Treasury. And the fact that Thomas Jefferson had a black mistress who bore him several children does not diminish the eloquence of the Declaration of Independence. Issues are different from the people who support them, and deserve to be judged on their own merits.

Name-calling and *argumentum ad hominem* are sometimes done with style. In the nineteenth-century when Lord John Russell became leader of the House of Commons, Disraeli remarked, "Now man may well begin to comprehend how the Egyptians worshipped an insect." But the best practitioner of name-calling in recent times was Winston Churchill. He once described fellow statesman Clement Attlee as "a modest man with much to be modest about," and, on another occasion, as "a sheep in sheep's clothing." Of political rival Stanley Baldwin, Churchill remarked, "He occasionally stumbles over the truth, but he always hastily picks himself up and hurries on as if nothing had happened." He punctured an arrogant political rival by murmuring as the man left the room, "There, but for the grace of God, goes God."

Where name-calling tries to get us to *reject* or *condemn* someone or something without examining the evidence, the glittering generality tries to get us to *accept* and *agree* without examining the evidence. The Institute for Propaganda Analysis calls glittering generalities "virtue words," and adds that every society has certain "virtue words" it feels deeply about. "Justice," "Motherhood," "the American Way," "Our Constitutional Rights," "Our Christian Heritage," are words many people in our society believe in, live by—and are willing to die for. "Let us fight to preserve our American Birthright!" cries the Congressman, and the crowd roars its approval. We might not be in favor of war, but who wants to go on record as being opposed to our "American Birthright"?

Glittering generalities have extraordinary power to move men. Condorcet, the great French leader, went to the guillotine for "Liberty, Equality, Fraternity!" He might not have gone so willingly had he known that the French Revolution was fought to establish the predominance of the bourgeoisie over the aristocracies, of the new-emerging capitalism over the surviving remnants of feudalism. Can anyone imagine Condorcet or any of the others like him giving up their lives for a cause stated in such terms? The struggle had to represent itself to men in glorious ringing terms to win their hearts and minds.

A glittering generality is very seductive and appealing, but when you open it up and look inside, it is usually empty. There is no specific, definable meaning. If you doubt that, try getting definitions from a dozen people and discover for yourself how widely the interpretations differ. Just what parts of the American society and culture does our "American Birthright" include? The Bill of Rights? The free enterprise system? The democratic process? The rights of citizens to bear arms? The rights of oil companies to fix prices? The rights of coal companies to strip the land? The rights of women to terminate their pregnancies? The rights of gays to equal employment? The rights of the government to limit these rights? All of the above? These glittering generalities are slippery creatures, all right. They can slide into almost any meaning. "We demand justice," say the workers, who mean that they want more money and the right to join a union. "*We* want justice" say the owners, who mean that they want the right to fire any worker who demands more money or the right to join a union.

In his Inaugural Address, President Carter announced the beginning of a "New Spirit" in the land, and asked us to dedicate ourselves to that spirit. What exactly is this "New Spirit" that he proclaimed? Where can one go to find it—much less dedicate one's self to it? Earlier, Carter also said, "We can have an American President who does not govern with negativism and fear of the future, but with vigor and vision and aggressive leadership—a President who is not isolated from our people, but who feels your pain and shares your dreams, and takes his strength and wisdom and courage from you." Well, we're all in favor of that. Clearly, then-President Gerald Ford would have heartily endorsed the very same sentiments. He was, after all, not running on a platform that promised he would be isolated from the people, ignore their pain and laugh at their dreams, or take from them only their weakness, ignorance, and cowardice.

In his satirical book, *Our Gang*, Philip Roth has President "Trick E. Dixon" defend his decision to go to war with Denmark because of the eleventh-century "expansionist policies" of Eric the Red, which, President Dixon says, clearly are in "direct violation of the Monroe Doctrine." The speech is a perfect example of how glittering generalities can be used to support any course of action, no matter how inane:

> I am certain . . . that the great majority of Americans will agree that the actions I have taken in the con-

frontation between the United States of America and the sovereign state of Denmark are indispensable to our dignity, our honor, our moral and spiritual idealism, our credibility around the world, the soundness of the economy, our greatness, our dedication to the vision of our forefathers, the human spirit, the divinely inspired dignity of man, our treaty commitments, the principles of the United Nations, and progress and peace for all people.

Now no one is more aware than I am of the political consequences of taking bold and forthright action in behalf of our dignity, idealism and honor, to choose just three. But I would rather be a one-term President and take these noble, heroic measures against the state of Denmark, than be a two-term President by accepting humiliation at the hands of a tenth-rate military power. I want to make that perfectly clear.[2]

There are times when fiction pales before reality. Trick E. Dixon's speech bears a startling resemblance to Richard M. Nixon's speech on August 23, 1972, the day he accepted the Republican nomination for President the second time. Here is how he defended his policy of continuing the war in Vietnam:

Let us reject . . . the policies of those who whine and whimper about our frustrations and call on us to turn inward. Let us not turn away from greatness. . . . With faith in God and faith in ourselves and faith in our country, let us have the vision and the courage to seize the moment and meet the challenge before it slips away.

On your television screens last night, you saw the cemetery in Leningrad I visited on my trip to the Soviet Union where 300,000 people died . . . during World War II. At the cemetery I saw the picture of a 12-year-old girl. She was a beautiful child. Her name was Tanya. I read her diary. It tells the terrible story of war. In the simple words of a child, she wrote of the deaths of the members of her family—Senya in De-

cember, Granny in January, then Yenka, then Uncle
Basha, then Uncle Leosha, then Mama in May.

And finally, these were the words in her diary: "All
are dead, only Tanya is left."

Let us think of Tanya and of the other Tanyas and
their brothers and sisters everywhere in Russia and in
China and in America as we proudly meet our responsibilities for leadership in the world in a way worthy of
a great people.

I ask you, my fellow Americans, to join . . . in
achieving a hope that mankind has had since the beginning of civilization.

Let us build a peace that our children and all the
children of the world can enjoy for generations to
come.

Tanya, touching as she is, has absolutely no relationship
whatever to our former policy in Vietnam. But that doesn't
matter. When it comes to politics, all that glitters is just
gabble.

Both name-calling and glittering generalities work by stirring emotions to befog thinking. Another approach is to create
a distraction, a "red herring" that will divert people's attention from the real issues. There are several different kinds of
red herrings that can be used effectively. Most effective is the
plain folks appeal. This is the verbal stratagem by which a
speaker tries to win confidence and support by appearing to
be "just one of the plain folks." "Wal, now, y'know I've
been a farm boy all my life," says the millionaire cattle ranch-
er to the crowd in Dallas. The same man speaking to a lun-
cheon of Wall Street bankers might be heard saying, "Now,
you know, I'm a businessman just like yourselves." Plain
folks is a favorite on the campaign trail, a proven vote-getter,
which is why so many candidates go around pumping factory
workers' hands, kissing babies in supermarkets, and sampling
pasta with Italians, fried chicken with Southerners, bagels
and blintzes with Jews.

Crowds love plain folks talk. When, during the Watergate

hearings, Senator Sam Ervin remarked, "Well, I'm sorry Senator Gurney does not approve of my method of examining the witness. I'm an old country lawyer, and I don't know the finer ways to do it," the audience went wild and it took five minutes to restore order in the room. Obviously, the people must not have been aware of Lyndon Johnson's famous quip that "Whenever I hear someone say, 'I'm just an old country lawyer,' the first thing I reach for is my wallet to make sure it's still there."

In the 1978 South Carolina Senate race, Strom Thurmond's main campaign document was a leaflet of "Family Recipes." "Estill pumpkin bread" and "Orangeburg hand cookies" won an easy victory over Democratic opponent Charles Ravenel, whose family boasted no such "down-home" cooking.

Anybody can get into the plain folks act with no trouble at all:

> I understand only too well that a world-wide distance separates Roosevelt's ideas and my ideas. Roosevelt comes from a rich family and belongs to the class whose path is smoothed. . . . I was only the child of a small, poor family and had to fight my way by work and industry. When the Great War came Roosevelt occupied a position where he got to know only its pleasant consequences, enjoyed by those who do business while others bleed. I was only one of those who carried out orders as an ordinary soldier, and naturally returned from the war just as poor as I was in the autumn of 1914. I shared the fate of millions, and Franklin Roosevelt only the fate of the so-called Upper Ten Thousand. . . . After the war, Roosevelt tried his hand at financial speculations. He made profits out of inflation, out of the misery of others, while I . . . lay in a hospital. . . .

That's Adolf Hitler speaking to the Reichstag after Germany declared war on America in 1941.

Another interesting red herring is *argumentum ad populum*,

more popularly known as "stroking." We all like to be liked, so it stands to reason that we will get nice, warm feelings about anybody who "strokes" or compliments us. It's nice to hear that we are "hardworking taxpayers" or "the most generous, free-spirited nation in the world." Farmers are told they are the "backbone of the American economy" and college students are hailed as the "leaders and policymakers of tomorrow." A truly gifted practitioner of *argumentum ad populum* can manage to stroke several different groups of people in the same breath. Here is how Philip Roth's Trick E. Dixon, in a speech that evokes memories of the famed "Checkers" television address, manages to cover as many bases as possible:

When I was a young, struggling lawyer, and Pitter [his wife] and I were living on nine dollars a week out in Prissier, California . . . I would read through my lawbooks and study long into the night in order to help my clients, most of whom were wonderful young people. . . . At that time, by the way, I had the following debts outstanding:

—$1,000 on our neat little house
   200 to my dear parents
   110 to my loyal and devoted brother
    15 to our fine dentist, a warmhearted Jewish man for whom we had the greatest respect
  4.35 to our kindly grocer, an old Italian who always had a good word for everybody. I still remember his name. Tony.
     5 cents to our Chinese laundryman, a slightly-built fellow who nonetheless worked long into the night over his shirts, just as I did over my lawbooks, so that his children might one day attend the college of their choice. I am sure they have grown up to be fine and outstanding Chinese-Americans.
    60 cents to the Polish man, or polack, as the Vice-President would affectionately call

him, who delivered the ice for our oldfashioned icebox. He was a strong man, with great pride in his native Poland.

We also owned monies amounting to $2.90 to a wonderful Irish plumber, a wonderful Japanese-American handyman and a wonderful couple from the deep South who happened to be of the same race as we were, and whose children played with ours in perfect harmony, despite the fact that they were from another region.[3]

A piquant variation of the stroking appeal is the "personal" letter which uses a computer to insert the recipient's name mechanically. The recipient is supposed to feel that the sender is saying all those nice things about him personally. Here's an interesting example:

Dear Mr. Hudgins:

The American Historical Society has created a flag in your honor. This flag commemorates the American Bicentennial and your Hudgins family name. Our research indicates that you are an affluent and achieving American family. You contribute to our society and pull your weight. . . . You are a winner. . . . You should see your Hudgins flag. We feel this flag finally gives your great name of Hudgins the recognition it so richly deserves. . . .

Presumably, the same compliments are being sent to people all over the United States. ("You should see your Kronkheit flag . . ." and "We feel this flag finally gives your great name of Ballsworth the recognition it so richly deserves.")

These advertise-by-mail manufacturers accurately pitch their sales to the political and emotional makeup of the consumer. They do it by studying the profiles of the kind of people who read *Ladies' Home Journal* or *Reader's Digest* or *Ms.* magazines or whatever subscription list they get the recipient's name from. Here's an example of a "stroking appeal" I recently received:

Dear Mrs. Cross

Frankly, you're someone magazines such as *Harper's*, *The New Yorker* and *Time* want as a subscriber. Judging from your neighborhood, you're far above average in means, intellect, and influence among those in the Syracuse and nearby areas.

. . . And when you think about it, Mrs. Cross, in just an hour or two a week, this is the most respected source for a busy intelligent person like yourself to keep informed on the events and ideas that affect our lives. . . .

There's something unsettling about having a computer say all those nice things about me. I'd invite him (it?) for dinner, but my stuffed cabbage might gum up his (its?) gears. Of course, all those flattering assumptions about my neighborhood, my income, my intellect, and my influence are machine-tooled and calculated to stroke me into a mood of warm acceptance. Not just me, obviously, but everyone else winnowed out from those all-knowing mailing lists as the kind who will be most susceptible to this particular sales pitch.

Another device that almost everyone is susceptible to is the transfer device, also known as "guilt or glory by association." In glory by association, the propagandist tries to "transfer" the positive feeling of something we love and respect over to the idea he wants us to accept. "Abraham Lincoln and Thomas Jefferson would have been proud of the Supreme Court decision to support school busing" is glory by association.

The process works equally well in reverse, when guilt by

association is used to transfer dislike or disapproval of one thing to an idea or group that the propagandist wants us to reject. "John Doe says we need to make some changes in the way our government operates. That's exactly what the Symbionese Liberation Army wants!" There's no logical connection between John Doe and the Symbionese Liberation Army apart from the one the propagandist is trying to create in our minds.

In a recent issue of *American Opinion* magazine, columnist Gary Allen comes out in favor of censorship of school textbooks, saying,

> Parents have been asked to pay and pay, but are told to leave the education of their children "to the experts. . . ." Adolf Hitler had his experts, often brilliant scholars with impressive degrees after their names, who prescribed curricula and textbooks designed to fashion the Nazi mind. In Moscow, there is a Ministry of Education composed of equally brilliant educational experts whose job it is to manipulate the minds of Soviet youth. . . .

The implication is that Nazi storm troopers and Russian secret agents are leagued in a dastardly plot to overthrow America by infiltrating our third-grade readers and spelling workbooks.

To illustrate the last of the red herring devices, consider the lemmings. Lemmings are arctic rodents with a queer habit: periodically, for reasons no one entirely understands, they mass together in a large herd and commit group suicide by rushing into deep water and drowning themselves. They run in blindly, and not one has been observed to stop, scratch its little head, and ask, "*Why* am I doing this? This doesn't look like such a great idea," and thus save itself from destruction.

Obviously, lemmings are driven to perform this strange mass-suicide rite by common instinct. People also choose to "Follow the herd," perhaps for more complex reasons, yet just as blindly. The *bandwagon* appeal capitalizes on people's urge to merge with the crowd.

Basically, the bandwagon appeal gets us to support an action or an opinion merely because it is popular—because "everyone else is doing it." Advertising relies heavily on the bandwagon appeal ("join the Pepsi people") but so do politicians ("Thousands of people have already shown their support by sending in a donation in the enclosed envelope. Won't you become one of us and work together to build a great America?")

The great success of the bandwagon appeal is evident in the various fashions and trends which capture the avid interest—and money—of thousands of people for a short time, then disappear utterly. "Oh, how I wish I could keep up with all the latest fashions as they go rushing by me into oblivion," English critic Max Beerbohm once wrote. Not so long ago, every child in North America wanted a coonskin cap so he could be like Davy Crockett. After that came the hula hoop and, more recently, the skateboard. Children are not the only group susceptible to bandwagon buying. Not so long ago, millions of adults rushed to the stores to buy their very own "pet rocks"—a concept silly enough to set even a lemming atwitter.

The fallacy of the bandwagon appeal is obvious. Just because everyone's doing something doesn't mean that it's worth doing. Large numbers of people have supported actions we now condemn. Dictators have risen to power in sophisticated and cultured countries with the support of millions of people who didn't want to be "left out" at the great historical moment. Once the bandwagon begins to move, momentum builds up dangerously fast.

If a propagandist can't reel you in by stirring your emotions or distracting your attention, he can always try a little faulty logic. This approach is more insidious than the other two because it gives the appearance of reasonable, fair argument. You have to look closely to see the holes in the logical fiber.

The most common kind of faulty logic is the false-cause-and-effect fallacy, also known as *post hoc, ergo propter hoc* ("after this, therefore because of this").

A good example of false-cause-and-effect reasoning is the story of the woman aboard the steamship *Andrea Doria*, who woke up from a nap and, feeling seasick, looked around for a call button to summon the steward to bring medication. She finally located a button on one of the walls of her cabin and pushed it. A split second later, the *Andrea Doria* collided with the *Stockholm* in the crash that was to send the ship to her destruction. "Oh, God, what have I done?" the woman screamed.

Her reasoning was understandable enough: a clear example of *post hoc, ergo propter hoc*. False-cause-and-effect reasoning can be persuasive because it *seems* so logical, or is confirmed by our own experience. "I swallowed X product—and my headache went away," says one woman. "We elected Y official—and unemployment went down," says another. We conclude, "There *must* be a connection." Maybe it would be good to keep in mind Harry Reasoner's remark, that "to call that cause and effect is to say that sitting in the third row of burlesque theatres is what makes men bald." Cause and effect is an awfully complex phenomenon; you need a good deal of evidence to prove that one event following another in time is, in fact, "caused" by the first.

False cause and effect is used—and with great effect—by our ever-reliable politicians. During the final weeks of the '76 campaign, Carter and Ford flooded the airwaves with their *post hoc, ergo propter hoc* messages. "Since I came to office," said Ford, "the inflation rate has dropped to 6%." "Since Gerald Ford took office," countered Carter, "the unemployment rate has risen 50% from 5.5% to 7.9%." Or how about this snip from a local political column for false-cause-and-effect reasoning:

> [Sex educators] loudly protest there is no relationship between their methods and promiscuity.

Yet the facts are disheartening, to say the least.

At a time when youngsters know more about sex than any preceding generation, we have more venereal disease, more teenage prostitution, more rape and generally, more sex-related problems than at any other time in history. If the advocates of sex education as now taught consider this an endorsement of their approach, then I think they're more in need of "instruction" than their childish charges.

Carry on with this reasoning and you can argue that the Boston Strangler, the Son of Sam, and the Zodiak Killer were all the monster creations of their ninth-grade hygiene classes. Of course, the writer blithely ignores all the multiple alternative possibilities for the phenomenon. It would be interesting to know whether the rate of venereal disease or of teenaged pregnancies increased following the publication of this column. Then, by the same reasoning, we could argue that the "disheartening" rise was hardly an endorsement of such "irresponsible" attacks upon the methods of the "sex educators."

Another tricky use of the false logic is the fallacy known as the *two-extremes dilemma*. Linguists have long noted that the English language tends to view reality in extreme or polar opposites. In English, things are either black or white, tall or short, up or down, front or back, left or right, good or bad, guilty or not guilty. "C'mon now, stop with all the talk—just give me a straightforward yes-or-no answer," we say, the understanding being that we will not accept anything in between. The problem is that there *are* things that can only be said in between; reality cannot always be dissected along strict lines. "Now, let's be fair," we say, "and listen to *both* sides of the argument." But who is to say that every argument has two sides? Can't there be a third—a fourth, fifth, or sixth—point of view? To say otherwise is to deny the nature of the world we live in, and accept the reality imposed by language.

In this statement by Lenin, the famed Marxist leader, we have a clear example of the two-extremes fallacy:

You cannot eliminate *one* basic assumption, one sub-
stantial part of this philosophy of Marxism [it is as if it
were a block of steel] without abandoning truth, without falling into the arms of bourgeois-reactionary
falsehood.

In other words, if you don't agree 100 percent with every
premise of Marxism, you do not pass go, but move directly to
jail for the ideological crime of "bourgeois-reactionary falsehood"—the other extreme of the political spectrum. There's
no option to be 99 3/4 percent in favor of Marxism, with perhaps a few quibbles about how a Communist state should be
administered. If you're not with it, you're agin it, and that's
that.

"Bourgeois reactionaries" are also capable of this kind of
faulty reasoning. Texas Senator John Tower, in his 1978 reelection campaign, stated, "I cast light on the issues; my opponent (Conservative Democrat Robert Krueger) plunges
them into darkness." A recent advertisement against gun control said, "If you're not helping to save hunting, you are helping to outlaw it." There is no place between these polar opposites for the millions of people in the world who might favor
hunting, but oppose handguns or Saturday night specials, or
even for those who might favor guns and yet oppose hunting,
not to mention all the gradations of opinion in between.

A famous example of the two-extremes dilemma is the slogan "America: Love it or leave it." The implicit suggestion is
that we must either accept *everything* in America today *just as
it is*—or get out. Of course, there's a whole range of action
and belief between those two extremes which the slogan entirely overlooks. The path of American history is littered with
slogans that display the two-extremes dilemma—"Fifty-four
forty or fight," "Better dead than Red," "Millions for defense but not one cent for tribute."

There's one more propaganda technique that's the most un-
derhanded of them all. It's called *card stacking*, and means
selecting only those facts—or falsehoods—which support the

propagandist's point of view, ignoring all others. For example, a candidate could be made to look like a legislative dynamo if you say, "Representative McNerd introduced more new bills than any other member of the Congress," and neglect to mention that most of them were so preposterous that they never got out of committee.

When we feel deeply about something, it's difficult to resist the temptation to stack the deck. Take this recent statement issued by an antiabortion group:

> Why does this sin-sick society show leniency toward murderers, rapists, robbers, and other vicious criminals and then does an about-face by wanting to destroy these little bundles of innocence through abortive murder: Let's face the truth. The majority of those who want to get rid of what God has created in their wombs are the unmarried who had a fling in the back seat of a parked automobile or some dingy motel room. Now when the price for a night of adventure is beginning to manifest itself, they want to add to their wickedness by slaying this innocent little baby. . . .

The Second Amendment Foundation, a group opposing gun control and an affiliate of the national gun lobby, recently published a small pamphlet "warning Americans against the dangers of gun confiscation," which includes the following dire forecast:

> Even though you may not own or have any direct interest in firearms, I believe you must be informed of the terribly serious consequences of what the liberal press refers to as "gun control."
>
> My friend, they are not talking about *control*, they want complete and total confiscation. This will mean the elimination and removal of *all police revolvers, all sporting rifles* and *target pistols* owned by law-abiding citizens.

Throughout our country a crime of violence, like murder, assault or rape, occurred once every 31 seconds in 1976. This means that over 1,026,280 men, women and children or elderly persons fell victims to thieves and hoodlums. . . .

Tell me, how high would the crime rate be if the criminal knew our police were unarmed? . . . I don't believe we can sit back and allow the "gun confiscation" people in this country to pass laws that would set the stage for the most terrifying crime wave ever to occur in modern history. . . .

No mention here that England and Japan, where guns are banned, have a much lower crime rate than the United States, or that the rate of homicides is dramatically less. That wouldn't fit into this carefully stacked deck. Nor would a contrary argument citing only the English and Japanese experience pass any test. For there might be any number of other explanations (see the *post hoc* fallacy) for that phenomenon. But never mind these picky details—the big picture is clear enough in the gun lobby pamphlet: vote for gun control, and if the bill passes, the next day every pervert and gangster in the city will be scratching at your windows and jimmying your door, while the police stand by helplessly, swatting them with their hats.

Card stacking was used shamelessly throughout the 1976 election campaign. In the New York State race, the "Democrats for Jim Buckley" came out with a campaign poster that announced:

Two thirds of all Democrats who voted in the recent primary did not vote for Moynihan. He won with a one percent margin. That's not what we call a party mandate. . . . So, what is there about Moynihan that turns off so many members of his own party?

A cleverly loaded question. Since there were four strong candidates running in the Democratic primary, it was well-nigh impossible for *anyone* to get anything approaching a "mandate." And the fact that the vote was so widely split among the candidates did not necessarily mean that anyone was "turned off" to Moynihan, just that they were "turned on" to other people. In the last weeks of the presidential race, Carter's people took out an ad that stated, "Today's inflation rate of 6% is higher than it was at any time between the Korean War and the Inauguration of Richard Nixon." True enough. But they neglected to mention that the inflation rate actually *dropped* from 12 percent to 6 percent during Ford's Administration—not the kind of omission that's likely to be an unconscious oversight. For their part, the Ford people came up with the remark that "This administration doesn't believe the way to end unemployment is to go to war." Of course, no one is depraved enough to suggest that the way to end unemployment is to go to war, but somehow that remark suggests that this may be what Carter had in mind.

Card stacking isn't necessarily *untrue*; it just isn't the whole truth. It's a bit reminiscent of the story about the three blind men who encountered an elephant one day. The first blind man felt the elephant's trunk and concluded he was confronted with a snake; the second felt the elephant's leg and decided it must be a tree trunk; the third felt the tusk and was convinced it was the antler of a deer. A skillful card stacker can take *part* of the truth and use it to argue for a particular issue and take another part to argue against the very same issue he just argued for. When one of his constituents wrote to him complaining about federal spending, Arizona Congressman Morris Udall replied tongue in cheek with this tour de force of card stacking:

> If, when you say "federal spending," you mean the billions of dollars wasted on outmoded naval shipyards and surplus airbases in Georgia, Texas and New York; if you mean the billions of dollars lavished at

Cape Kennedy and Houston on a "moondoggle" our nation cannot afford; if, sir, you mean the $2-billion wasted each year in wheat and corn price supports which rob midwestern farmers of their freedoms and saddle taxpayers with outrageous costs of storage in already bulging warehouses . . . if you mean the bloated federal aid to education schemes calculated to press federal educational controls down upon every student in this nation; if you mean the $2-billion misused annually by our Public Health Service and National Institutes of Health on activities designed to prostitute the medical profession and foist socialized medicine on every American; if, sir, you mean all these ill-advised, unnecessary federal activities which have destroyed state's rights, created a vast, ever-growing, empire-building bureaucracy regimenting a once free people by the illusory bait of cradle-to-grave security, and which indeed have taken us so far down the road to socialism that it may be, even at this hour, too late to retreat—then I am unyielding, bitter and foursquare in my opposition, regardless of the personal or political consequences.

But, on the other hand, if when you say "federal spending," you mean those funds which maintain Davis Monthan Air Force Base, Fort Huachuca and other Arizona defense installations so vital to our nation's security, and which every year pour hundreds of millions of dollars into our state's economy . . . if you mean those funds to send our brave astronauts voyaging, even as Columbus, into the unknown, in order to guarantee that no aggressor will ever threaten these great United States by nuclear blackmail from outer space; if you mean those sound farm programs which insure our hardy Arizona cotton farmers a fair price for their fiber, protect the sanctity of the family farm, ensure reasonable prices for consumers, and put to work for all the people of the world the miracle of American agricultural abundance . . . if you mean the federal education funds which built desperately

needed college classrooms and dormitories for our local universities, provide little children in our Arizona
schools with hot lunches (often their only decent meal
of the day), furnish vocational training for our high
school youth, and pay $10-million in impact funds to
relieve the hard-pressed Arizona school property taxpayers from the impossible demands created by the
presence of large federal installations; if you mean the
federal medical and health programs which have eradi-
cated the curse of malaria, small-pox, scarlet fever
and polio from our country, and which even now enable dedicated teams of scientists to close in merci-
lessly on man's age-old enemies of cancer, heart disease, muscular dystrophy, multiple sclerosis, and
mental retardation that afflict our little children, senior
citizens and men and women in the prime years of life;
if you mean all these federal activities by which a free
people in the spirit of Jefferson, Lincoln, Teddy Roo-
sevelt, Wilson and FDR, through a fair and progres-
sive income tax, preserve domestic tranquility and
promote the general welfare while preserving all our
cherished freedoms and our self-reliant national character, then I shall support them with all the vigor at my
command.[4]

Perhaps a good way to wind up is to show you how all these
propaganda devices, from name-calling through card stacking, can be put to work together. Let's take a local candidate
who doesn't have any very good reason why people should
vote for him instead of his opponent, so he's going to have to
rely on propaganda and not reasoned argument. Here, then, is
State Senator Al Yakalot, running for reelection to the State
Senate, addressing a crowd of his constituents on election
day:

Speech by Senator Yakalot to His Constituents

My dear friends and fellow countrymen in this great and
beautiful town of Gulliville, I stand before you today as your

candidate for State Senator. And before I say anything else, I want to thank you wonderful people, you hardworking, right-living citizens that make our country great, for coming here today to hear me speak. Now, I'm at a disadvantage here because I don't have the gift of gab that a big-city fella like my opponent has—I'm just a small-town boy like you fine people—but I'm going to try, in my own simple way, to tell you why you should vote for me, Al Yakalot.

Now, my opponent may appear to you to be a pretty nice guy, but I'm here today to tell you that his reckless and radical policies represent a dire threat to all that we hold dear. He would tear down all that is great and good in America and substitute instead his own brand of creeping socialism.

For that's just what his ridiculous scheme to set up a hot meal program for the elderly in this town amounts to—socialism. Sure, *he* says our local citizens have expressed their willingness to donate some of their time and money to a so-called senior citizens' kitchen. But this kind of supposed "volunteer" work only undermines our local restaurants—in effect, our private enterprise system. The way I see it, in this world a man's either for private enterprise or he's for socialism. Mr. Stu Pott, one of the leading strategists of the hot meal campaign (a man who, by the way, sports a Fidel Castro beard) has said the program would be called the "Community Food Service." Well, just remember that the words "Community" and "Communism" look an awful lot alike!

After all, my friends, our forefathers who made this country great never had any free hot meal handouts. And look at what they did for our country! That's why I'm against the hot meal program. Hot meals will only make our senior citizens soft, useless, and dependent.

And that's not all you should know about my opponent, my fellow citizens. My pinko opponent has also called for a "consumers crusade" against what he terms "junk food" in school lunches. By "junk food," he means things like potato chips and hot dogs. Potato chips and hot dogs! My friends, I say that we've raised generations of patriotic American children on potato chips and hot dogs and we're not about to stop now! Potato chips have been praised by great Americans as well as by leading experts on nutrition.

What's more, potato chips are good for our children, too. A recent study shows that after children were given lunches that often included potato chips, their energy and attention spans improved by over ten percent. Obviously, potato chips have a beneficial effect on children's ability to learn. My opponent has tried to tell you that his attack on the venerable American custom of potato chip eating is just an attempt to improve our children's health and beauty. Yet this plan is supported by Congresswoman Doris Schlepp, who is no beauty herself!

My fellow taxpayers, I'm here today to tell you that this heartless plot to deprive our little ones of the food that they need most and love best won't work, because it's just plain unworkable. Trying to discourage children from eating potato chips is like trying to prevent people from voting—and the American people just aren't going to stand for it!

I'm mighty grateful to all you wonderful folks for letting me speak what is in my heart. I know you for what you are—the decent, law-abiding citizens that are the great pulsing heart and the lifeblood of this, our beloved country. I stand for all that is good in America, for our American way and our American Birthright. More and more citizens are rallying to my cause every day. Won't you join them—and me—in our fight for America?

Thank you and May God Bless You All.

10

Now What?

Books have to be read. It is the only way of discovering what they contain. A few savage tribes eat them, but reading is the only method of assimilation revealed to the West.

E. M. Forster

I am the King of Rome, and above grammar.
Sigismund, at the Council of Constance

A few years ago, a freshman student came into my office to discuss a paper he had written for my course. He was a college student, yet he was writing at no better than seventh-grade level. I asked him what the last book he had read was.

"I've never read a book," he said.

Incredible as it may seem, in twelve years of school, including four years of high school, he literally had never read a book. In ninth grade, he had taken an elective course called Issues and Answers, and the teacher never assigned any books to read. "We just sat around and rapped about capital punishment and abortion—you know, that stuff." In tenth grade, he took a course in history of film. There was a book assigned for that course, but the teacher never gave tests so he had never had to read it. I wrote out a list of books he might want to read someday *if* he ever felt like it. He thanked me courteously and left, leaving me to ponder the inanities of a system that purports to educate someone without ever requiring him to read a book.

Two years later, when he was about to graduate from community college, he returned to see me. Somewhere along the line, he had gotten fired up enough to dig out my recommended reading list, and had gone to the library and taken out *The Catcher in the Rye* by J. D. Salinger. He came back to tell me he had started the book and was enjoying it, but there was an important question that he wanted to ask.

"Fire away," I said.

"I just wanted to know if when you're reading a book and you get to a real good section, can you turn ahead a few pages to see what happens?"

If I had ever doubted what he had told me two years before, I couldn't any longer. Here was a young man, nineteen years old, who had never read a book, who didn't even know the simple mechanics of book reading, coming to me for advice on how to approach this arcane art form.

"Pete," I said, "it's your book and you can read it any way you like. It's not like TV or a movie. Lots of people look ahead to see what's going to happen when they're reading a book. I do it myself all the time."

"Oh, thank you," he said, relieved to know that he wasn't violating some sacred code of the Society of English Teachers and Book Readers.

Pete graduated that summer and went on to a four-year college where he plans to get his B.A. and perhaps an M.A. in business administration. I hope the pleasure he gets from *The Catcher in the Rye* will stay with him, and that he will read many more books. But maybe he won't. Maybe in a few years he'll be telling someone that he's read *one* book in his entire life, which sounds like the old joke about the man who went into a bookstore one day to get out of the rain. The clerk asked him if he would like a book. "What for, lady?" the man asked. "I've already got a book!"

Of course, Pete isn't the problem. The problem is the millions of Petes. Today, twenty-six million Americans cannot read well enough to understand stop signs and other simple directions. They can't read help-wanted ads or the telephone directory, the directions on a bottle of medicine, or decipher Social Security and driver's license forms. They are functionally illiterate. Millions of other Americans who are not illiterate are nonetheless crippled by poor reading skills.

A high-school diploma no longer carries a guarantee of literacy. All that is required to graduate from high school these days is eighth-grade reading skills. Increasingly, students can't even meet that criterion. In 1976, 1542 New York City high-school students were denied diplomas because they couldn't read at the eighth-grade level. Even those who do graduate may not be able to read at that level. At the City University of New York, close to fifty percent of all entering freshmen are only capable of reading below the eighth-grade level. Recently, the chancellor of the University of Illinois in Chicago said that nineteen percent of the freshmen at his university could manage nothing more sophisticated than an eighth-grade reader. More chillingly, many students who could read only at sixth- to eighth-grade level ranked in the *top* half of their high-school classes!

Part of the reason for this shocking semiliteracy is a growing distrust of books. A few months ago, our mail carrier saw a girl carrying a book and remarked, "I stay away from that reading stuff. Boy, books can really mess up your mind!" His attitude is typical of many young people today—that words are the enemies of real and meaningful experience. It is also the attitude of many in the new breed of film directors, like Nicholas Roeg and Brian di Palma, who deride words and contend that their work is judged unfairly because critics have been reared in a narrow "literary tradition." To them, visual imagery is all—to the point where the image replaces verbal meaning. Life simply moves too fast for words to keep up, and all those words in books take too much time to get through. As syndicated columnist Bob Greene says, "In a disposable age, the book for keeping and re-reading is an anachronism, a ponderous dinosaur in a high-speed society."

What are the social effects of this decline in reading skills?

For one: there is a loss in the ability to understand and analyze complex ideas. For another: there is a loss in the ability to *express* ideas. As the ability to read declines, so does the ability to write.

Anyone who teaches English today knows that most students can't write. Their writing skills have been in a steady downward spiral since the mid-sixties. "Composition is more of a problem today than it was ten or fifteen years ago," says Remington Patterson, acting dean of the faculty at Barnard College. "The good students now write as well as those of previous years, but the poor writers are more numerous and poorer." At Stanford University, one of the nation's best-rated schools, an English professor recently estimated that "seventy-five percent of our entering freshmen are unprepared to do college-level writing." At Berkeley, another fine school, over fifty percent of freshmen's writing skills are so weak they must take courses in remedial English.

The most damning evidence of the decline in writing skills comes from the precipitous drops in student scores on the SAT, or Scholastic Aptitude Test, which measures verbal and reasoning abilities. The SAT is taken by more than one million college-bound students every year. Over the last twelve years, the average scores on the verbal section of the test have declined 38 points, from 478 to 434 out of a possible 800. "And it's not as if these tests are rigorously demanding," says a spokesman for the agency that administers the SAT. "Anyone with even a basic literacy should be able to do well on them." Here, for example, are two representative questions a student might find on an SAT exam:

> The sentence below has two blanks, each blank indicating that something has been omitted. Beneath the sentence are five lettered sets of words. Choose the set of words that best fits the meaning of the sentence as a whole:

"From the first the islanders, despite an outward
———, did what they could to ——— the ruthless oc-
cupying power."

A) harmony . . . assist   D) resistance . . . destroy
B) enmity . . . embarrass E) acquiescence . . . thwart
C) rebellion . . . foil

Any student who plans to do college-level studies should be
able to recognize that the answer is E. Another kind of question asked on the SAT tests word comprehension by asking
the student to identify antonyms, as in this question:

Choose the word that is most clearly *opposite* in meaning to the word in capital letters:

COMPOSURE:
A) analysis   D) agitation
B) alertness   E) destruction
C) contrast

Again, the answer, D, should be easy for a high-school graduate. Notice that these questions are not testing for the niceties
of grammar. No one expects (or even wants) students to be as
punctilious as Dominic Boubours, the French grammarian
who in 1702 remarked on his deathbed, "I am about to—or I
am going to—die; either expression is correct." An apocry-
phal story about Dr. Samuel Johnson, the famous lexicogra-
pher, shows that he had the same regard for fine distinctions
of speech: When his wife caught him in the arms of another
woman and cried, "Sir, I am surprised," Johnson supposedly
answered, "Madam, *I* am surprised; *you* are astonished."

The SAT tests only for basic literacy, for an understanding
of words and their meaning. Increasingly, students are unable
to fit words to their meaning. Examples of this "word-sense
aphasia" abound in student papers. These interesting ones
were collected by Temple Porter:

> Henry VIII found walking difficult because he had an abbess on his knee.

> In Mrs. Warren's Profession, her profession is the Oldest Profession, but she is not really a Lost Woman. She is just mislaid.

> Abstinence is a good thing if practiced in moderation.[1]

Words have lost their moorings and are afloat in a sea of confusion. Even when students don't confuse word meanings they reveal a disturbing bias toward inanity. The following sentences make sense of a sort, though not exactly the sort intended:

> Today every Tom, Dick, and Harry is named Bill.

> A virgin forest is a place where the hand of man has never set foot.

> In A Street Car named Desire, the climax is when Blanche goes to bed with Stella's husband.

> It was the painter Donatello's interest in the female nude that made him the Father of the Renaissance.

The decline in writing skills among students extends even to the time-honored practice of forging notes from parents to excuse absence from class. Some recent examples that weren't exactly persuasive:

> My son is under Doctor's care and should not take P.E. Please execute him.

> John has been absent because he had two teeth taken out of his face.

> Please excuse Roland from P.E. for a few days. Yesterday he fell out of a tree and misplaced his hip.

Please excuse Sarah for being absent. She was sick and I had her shot.[2]

Recently, the National Assessment of Educational Progress conducted a five-year study during which it analyzed essays written by high-school students. Predictably, they found students often weak in grammar, spelling, and punctuation. More seriously, they found students were unable to shape a coherent thought. I have found this true of students' speech as well as of their writing. Recently I was talking to a seventeen-year-old, who mentioned that she really hated a girl named Ellen who went to her school.

"Oh, really?" I asked. "What don't you like about her?"

"Well . . . well . . . she's just kinda . . . she's kinda—you know, she's the type of girl that . . . you know, she's really, aaahhh— Ooh, I don't know, there's just something about her that I really don't like, y'know what I mean?"

No, I didn't know what she meant, I wonder if *she* knew what she meant, for she had such a hard time putting it into words. The collapse of coherence is a signature of the time. As an English professor friend of mine asks, "How can people form vital human bonds if they haven't the words, if they can't express what they feel? How can they conduct the ordinary affairs of everyday life without the right words?"

His concern is not overstated, because the statistics are real: verbal skills are weakening within all ethnic groups, all socioeconomic classes, in private schools as well as in public schools. It's no longer only minorities or the underprivileged who cannot read or write—as if that weren't bad enough. Now our middle-class kids are two to three grades behind in their reading skills; middle-class kids cannot articulate their ideas.

A paper recently turned in by one of my students, a young man from an upper-middle-class background, who has attended "good" private schools since the eighth grade, provides an example. The student had two weeks to complete the writing assignment and he had a choice of seven topics, including the option of writing on anything he wished. The topic he chose asked for a definition of an abstract concept like Happiness or Truth or Freedom, giving a series of concrete illustrations. The assignment was thoroughly discussed and explained in class, and several examples of how to proceed were given. Here is what the student wrote:

Love is Happy

to be in Love is to be very happy. Love
is a very special thing. Just think if
we could spread Love around like a disease
the world would be so different. the world
would be so happy.

To be in Love is to be very happy, cause
once in Love always will be in Love. Love
is very sacred. Love is never have to say
"I'm sorry." When two people are in Love
they see things other people don't, like
real honest-to-good happiness. What is
this real honest to good happiness? Well
it's being in Love and very happy with
each other. Never keeping things from
each other and always being honest, cause
honesty is the best policy.

Just think if we could spread Love around!
If Love was spread around everybody would
be happy and the world would be at peace
and no body would have to worry about any
takeovers in the government. The people
would band all artillery and put everything
they got into medcine and science to improve ourselves as humans. If love was
spread out, people could work together.

The feelings in Love are and really should

be happy feelings. Love is kind. But
nobody could live on Love alone. To be in
Love is happy, but to be happy doesn't mean
your in Love. Happiness has nothing to do
with Love, but Love has a lot of things to
do with happiness. The love with your
family should be a happy love, a strong
and braceful love. People should never
get lust mixed up with the real Love.

End

Cambridge professor Arthur Quiller-Couch once wrote, "If your language is confusion, your intellect, if not your whole character, will almost certainly correspond." Style, as Buffon said, is the man.

Slaughtering the King's English is not a practice limited only to students. An alarming number of people in all walks of life habitually murder the English language, without any inkling of the gravity of the crime they are committing. Recently, some bright soul dipped into the files of the letters written by citizens to the U.S. Department of Health, Education, and Welfare. He emerged with some delightful examples of how words can be allowed to stray from their intended meaning:

I am glad to report that my husband who is missing is dead.

I am very much annoyed to find that you have branded my son an illiterate. This is a dirty lie, as I was married a week before he was born.

Mrs. Jones hasn't had any clothes for a year and has been visited regularly by the clergy.

You have changed my little boy to a girl. Will this make any difference?

In answer to your letter, I have given birth to a boy weighing ten pounds. I hope that is satisfactory.

I am forwarding my marriage certificate and my 3 children, one of which is a mistake as you can see.

In accordance with your instructions, I have given birth to twins in the enclosed envelope.

Some have achieved a kind of public distinction for the way they manhandle the English language. Baseball manager Casey Stengel's speech was so unusual it even acquired a name of its own—"Stengelese." This was, as Charles Maher of *The New York Times* has said, "a convoluted tongue, unencumbered by grammatical rules and beyond diagramming." Two choice examples:

"That feller runs splendid but he needs help at the plate which coming from the country chasing rabbits all winter give him strong legs despite he broke one falling out of a tree which shows you can't tell and when a curveball comes he waves at it and if pitchers don't throw curves you have no pitching staff so how is a manager to know whether to tell boys to fall out of trees and break legs so he can run fast even if he can't hit a curveball?"

"I would be batting the big feller if they wasn't ready with the other one, but a left-hander would be the thing if they wouldn't have knowed it already because there is more things involved than could come up on the road, even after we've been home for a long while."

Another sports figure who bids fair to pick up the banner of fractured English is Coach Bill Peterson of the Houston Oilers. Once Peterson said of the Oakland Raiders, "That Oakland is tough. They timidate your offense, they timidate your defense, they even timidate the officials." When discussing strategy one day, Peterson confessed, "We're changing our floormat this week." (Presumably if he didn't it would be curtains for the team.) In the locker room as the first game of the season was about to begin, he told his team, "We are all in this together, and don't you remember it." A few minutes later, as they were about to kick off, he cheered them on with this immortal speech: "Men, I want you thinking of just one word all season. One word and only one word: Super Bowl!" The late movie producer Samuel Goldwyn showed the same confusion in reverse when he answered someone in "just two words—im-possible!"

At least when Andrei Gromyko of the Soviet Union commented to a *New York Times* reporter that "a lot of water has flown under the bridge since the war," he had the excuse that he was speaking a foreign language. But why do our own professional journalists and writers insist on treating English as a foreign language? When the Duke of Windsor died, one newspaper described the Duchess as "a grievous widow." In an article about science fiction writer Isaac Asimov, author of over a hundred books, one reviewer wrote: "[Asimov] attributes his profligacy to the fact that he can type 90 words a minute." And Pierre Salinger, President John Kennedy's own press secretary, earned an "Et tu, Brute" award when he described him as "a vociferous reader."

What has caused this growing illiteracy? Educators point to several different culprits. Television is the one most often cited. Columnist George Will notes, "Disparagement of television is second only to watching television as an American pastime." Indisputably, watching television is *the* American pastime. The average eighteen-year-old has spent between fifteen and twenty thousand hours in front of the tube. That's the equivalent of more than two full years of his life! At age eighteen, he has spent only eleven thousand hours in school, which means that he receives up to twice as many hours of "instruction" from TV as from teachers or books. And what programs do teenagers watch? The Nielsen ratings for a typical week in October 1978 listed the top ten programs among teen-aged viewers: *Three's Company, Mork and Mindy, Happy Days,*

Barney Miller, Taxi, The ABC Sunday Night Movie, Soap, Battlestar Galactica, Laverne and Shirley, and *Charlie's Angels.* Whatever their value as entertainment, none of these qualifies as a valuable instructional resource.

The real danger of TV, though, is not in the quality of the programming. Marshall McLuhan said it years ago, and it's true in an even more pernicious sense today: the medium *is* the message. The "message" of TV viewing is that it's unnecessary to *do* anything; you can have all the friends and entertainment you want with a flick of the switch. If those friends begin to bore you, there's another group waiting for you on another channel. This is the lesson children learn every time they plop down in front of the TV. A *New Yorker* cartoon a few years back foresaw the final result of this kind of conditioning: The cartoon shows a man trying to fix a flat tire in pouring rain. His two kids are inside the car, looking out the window grumpily, and the man is explaining to them, "Don't you understand? We *can't* turn to another channel. This is real life!!"

Is habitual TV viewing really so bad for children? The answer is yes. TV watching is essentially a nonverbal, right-hemisphere activity. The speech center is in the left hemisphere of the brain, and children need stimulation of the left hemisphere to build verbal skills. So children who watch a lot of TV grow up without having developed the cerebral capacity to verbalize effectively. Recent tests of children who have been exposed to massive doses of TV confirm this diagnosis.

The temptation is great to use the TV as a baby-sitter. A child may begin watching TV at seven in the morning and sit through hour after hour of Captain Kangaroo and Batman and Robin and Isis and commercials for Flintstone vitamins and Count Chocula cereal and other goodies, and she will learn to recite the virtues of Electra Woman and tell you why Blue Bonnet margarine is better than the other leading brand. But she *cannot* read, she *cannot* play creatively on her own, and she *cannot* tell you why she doesn't like her first-grade art teacher. There are children all over the country even now sitting passively in front of the TV set, watching and hearing, but not *producing* language. And that is going to be—no, it already is—a serious problem. Leslie Perelman, a professor of linguistics, says, "The only way you learn to speak a language is to speak it; mere passive listening will not make a child a competent language producer."

Nor does watching television stimulate a child's imagination. After months and years of television watching, children are literally bereft of imaginative sources of play. Turn off the television set and they don't seem to have any idea of what to do next! They don't even have the desire to get up and play a game, or get toys, or go out to see friends. They sit there whining that they're bored. It's almost as if watching the tube drains them of all creativity, of the will to live their own lives instead of seeing make-believe people live make-believe lives.

TV is not the only villain. Our educational system is also to blame. Back in the 1960s, when student alienation and hostility to "the system" was at its peak, there was a move to "liberate" classrooms from the strictures of formal study. Edward Hall, English teacher at the Hill School, says the decade of the sixties saw the birth of four new principles of learning: "Learning should always be fun," "I teach what I want," "Let the students choose," and "If it's new, it's good." Some of this liberation may have been a good thing. Too many generations of schoolchildren had been tyrannized by schoolmarms who reduced the study of the English language to petty grammatical distinctions—when to use "shall" instead of "will"—and who called a child's entire character into question if he used a preposition at the end of a sentence. They were part of what someone has called, mockingly, "a veritable whom's whom of grammarians." (Winston Churchill once wrote to an editor who had rewritten one of his sentences to avoid a final preposition, "This is the kind of arrant pedantry up with which I shall not put.")

In the sixties, professional sentiment turned away from

"arbitrary and repressive rules" and there began a new era of permissiveness in education. In time, however, the momentum carried them too far. Too many teachers began to confuse liberation—which requires a certain amount of self-discipline and structure—with license. "There was a philosophy that education should take the form of a massage parlor that makes the students feel good," says Roderick Park, dean of the College of Letters and Sciences at Berkeley. "I think this resulted in a decline in fundamental writing and math skills."

In the sixties, less and less writing was taught in schools. Students didn't "like" learning to write as much as they "liked" learning about science fiction, or movies, or the history of the comic books—so nobody bothered to teach writing anymore; it was, in the vocabulary of the times, "irrelevant." Rap sessions, full of loose talk and sloppy ideas, took the place of formal debating; "free writing," in which spelling and grammar were never corrected (to avoid stifling the cretive spirit), replaced essays and reports and sentence diagraming. The standard writing and literature courses decreased in number, and were superseded by a slew of new, "fun" courses: Women and Literature, History of the Film, TV as Pop Culture, and the like. Phyllis Zagano, a professor of English, says, "I once asked my college students to describe their high-school curricula. They had studied everything from building sets for theater to yoga, but no one had had a course even faintly resembling rhetoric." Gene Lyons, writer and teacher, summarizes the inevitable result: "American students are not learning to write because nobody bothers to teach them how."

Some teachers stopped teaching the fundamentals of writing because of political convictions. Dr. Richard Ohmann, Wesleyan professor and editor of the *College English Journal*, argues that teaching "correct" English is largely a matter of serving the Establishment and maintaining the status quo. He feels that English teachers should encourage students to write in their own dialects and thus "act as allies of the socialist revolution." This attitude finds a surprising degree of support within the profession. In 1972, the National Council of Teachers of English drafted a statement entitled "The Students' Right to Their Own Language," which argues that Standard English is just a dialect like any other, and that insistence upon its use is an act of repression by the dominant white middle class. "Linguistic snobbery was tacitly encouraged by a slavish reliance on rules," the statement reads, "and these attitudes had consequences far beyond the realm of language." It is true that no dialect or form of speech is inherently "better" than any other; any dialect serves its purpose if meaning is effectively communicated. But even if Standard English is no "better" than any other, even if it is the "prestige" dialect the dissenters deplore, the hard fact is it's the principal dialect in America today. It is the language used in literature and commerce, law and government, medicine and science, and throughout the infinitely complex power structure of American society. That being the case, children who do not learn how to use Standard English—to speak it and write it when they need to—are sentenced to live outside the power structure. This was certainly the view of a group of black parents in Louisiana, who protested that their children were being deprived of a quality education because they were being taught that grammar and precision in writing did not matter. To them, a "quality education" was equated with writing and speaking in the way that more affluent white people did.

Fortunately, the recent distrust of the written word seems to be on the wane. Dismayed by the deterioration in students' ability to write, school administrators across the country are establishing programs to improve the teaching of composition before the decline goes too far. As J. Mitchell Morse says, he can see the "handwriteing on the wall" [sic]—and it's misspelled. In colleges, there is a growing emphasis on writing instead of on traditional literature courses. "Writing is the most important thing we can teach," says Harry Levin, dean of the College of Arts and Sciences at Cornell. Cornell became the first university in the country to appoint a full-time dean of writing, a precedent that other institutions are likely to follow. Colleges everywhere are reinstating freshman composition programs that were eliminated in the sixties. Harvard University has set up a new Writing Center where students can go to get help with their writing skills.

Let us hope that this turnabout has come in time. For what is at stake is not simply a generation of young people who cannot organize a paragraph. "Learning to write is the hardest, most important thing any child does," says Carlos Baker, chairman of English at Princeton. "Learning to write is learning to think." It is words that give coherence to the billion bits of information that fill our brains, and if we lose the knack of stringing them together, then the business of communication is going to be a bit tricky. "You just don't know anything until you can write it," says S. I. Hayakawa, Senator from California, and a famous semanticist. "Sure you can argue things in your head and bring them out at cocktail parties, but in order to argue anything thoroughly, you must be able to write it down on paper." In order to understand the world we live in, we must first be able to describe it.

Central to the very idea of democracy is the concept of an informed and educated people. The more informed and educated they are, the better chance democracy has to survive. And how else can they be informed and educated save through the medium of words? Consider the words of Aldous Huxley, who believed language should be used not to control man, but to set him free:

> Children should be taught that words are indispensable . . . the only begetters of all civilization, all science, all consistency of high purpose . . . and the only begetters at the same time of all superstition, all collective madness and stupidity, all the dismal historical succession of crimes in the name of God, King, Nation, Party, Dogma . . . To those who think that

liberty is a good thing, and that it may some day be possible for people to live in a society fit for free, fully human individuals, a thorough education in the nature of language, its uses and abuses, seems indispensable.[3]

Amen.

Notes

Chapter 1

1. Suzanne K. Langer, "Signs and Symbols in Language and Thought." Excerpt from Langer, "Lord of Creation." *Fortune*, January 1944.

2. Helen Keller, *The Story of My Life*. New York: Doubleday, 1936.

3. "Fenimore Cooper's Literary Offenses." In *The Complete Humorous Sketches and Tales of Mark Twain*, Charles Neider, ed. New York: Doubleday, 1961.

Chapter 2

1. Sidney Harris, *Town and Country News*, November 28, 1974.

2. Peter Berger, "The Briefing." In *Pouring Down Words*, S. H. Elgin, ed. Englewood Cliffs: Prentice-Hall, 1975.

3. Stuart Chase, "Gobbledygook." In *Power of Words*, New York: Harcourt Brace Jovanovich, 1953.

4. Neil Postman, *Crazy Talk, Stupid Talk*. New York: Delacorte, 1976.

5. James L. Konski, "The Bicycle Anarchy." *Transportation Engineering* 99, no. TE4, November 1973.

6. "A Cure for the Blues." In *The Complete Humorous Sketches and Tales of Mark Twain*.

7. John Simon, "Why Reed Can't Write." *More* magazine, March 1977.

8. Russell Baker, "Little Miss Muffet." In *Poor Russell's Almanac*. New York: Doubleday, 1972.

Chapter 3

1. Alexander Cockburn, "How to Earn Your Trench Coat." In *Stop the Presses, I Want to Get Off!*, Richard Pollak, ed. New York: Random House, 1975.

2.——, "Death Rampant." In Pollak, *Stop the Presses*.

3. Ibid.

4. Marya Mannes, "What's Wrong With Our Press?" In *Journalism*, Allen and Linda Kirshner, eds. New York: Odyssey Press.

5. Ron Nessen, "Too Much Trivia, Too Little Substance." *TV Guide*, March 12, 1977.

6. Eric Levin, "How the Networks Decide What the News Is." *TV Guide*, July 2, 1977.

7. See note 5.

Chapter 5

1. Mark Twain, "The Awful German Language." In *The Complete Humorous Sketches and Tales of Mark Twain*.

2. Rudolf Flesch, *The Art of Clear Thinking*. New York: Harper and Row, 1951.

3. William Espy, *An Almanac of Words at Play*. New York: Clarkson N. Potter, 1975.

4. Alleen Pace Nilsen, "Sexism in Children's Books and

Elementary Teaching Materials." In *Sexism and Language*, Alleen Pace Nilsen et al. eds. National Council of Teachers of English, Urbana, Illinois, 1977.

5. Muriel Rukeyser, "Oedipus Myth Revisited." In Nilsen et al., *Sexism and Language*.

Chapter 6

1. David Ogilvy, *Confessions of an Advertising Man*. New York: Atheneum, 1963.

2. Ashley Montagu, *Anatomy of Swearing*. New York: Macmillan, 1973.

3. H. L. Mencken, *The American Language*. New York: Alfred Knopf, 1936, 1960.

4. Harry Whewell, "The Crisis in Swearing." In *Anatomy of Swearing*.

5. Edward Sagarin, *The Anatomy of Dirty Words*. New York: Lyle Stuart, 1962.

6. John Brophy and Eric Partridge. In *Anatomy of Swearing*.

7. Wayland Young. In *Anatomy of Swearing*.

8. *Anatomy of Swearing*, p. 14.

9. *Anatomy of Swearing*, p. 300.

Chapter 7

1. Herbert Otto and Roberta Otto, *Total Sex*. New York: Peter H. Wyden, 1972.

2. Evelyn Waugh, *The Loved One*. Boston: Little, Brown, 1948.

Chapter 8

1. Russell Baker. In *Words at Play*.

2. Frank Sullivan, *A Pearl in Every Oyster*. New York: Grosset & Dunlap, Universal Library, 1962, pp. 46, 289.

3. ———. *The Night the Old Nostalgia Burned Down.* New York: Grosset & Dunlap, Universal Library, 1961.

4. Arlan J. Large. In *Words at Play*, p. 285.

5. John Beaudouin and Everett Mattlin, *The Phrase-Droppers Handbook.* New York: Doubleday, 1976.

6. Cyra McFadden, *The Serial: A Year in the Life of Marin County.* New York: Alfred Knopf, 1977.

Chapter 9

1. Peter Farb, *Word Play.* New York: Alfred Knopf, 1974.

2. Philip Roth, *Our Gang.* New York: Random House, 1971.

3. *Our Gang.*

4. Morris Udall. In Richard Altick, *Preface to Critical Reading.* New York: Holt, Rinehart and Winston, 1969.

Chapter 10

1. Temple Porter. In *Words at Play.*

2. *American Educator*, spring 1978.

3. Aldous Huxley, "Education on a Non-Verbal Level." *Daedalus*, spring 1962.